AQA Spanish

AS

Grammar Workbook

Chris Fuller

OXFORD
UNIVERSITY PRESS

Great Clarendon Street, Oxford, OX2 6DP, United Kingdom

Oxford University Press is a department of the University of Oxford. It furthers the University's objective of excellence in research, scholarship, and education by publishing worldwide. Oxford is a registered trade mark of Oxford University Press in the UK and in certain other countries

First published by Nelson Thornes Ltd in 2013
This edition published by Oxford University Press in 2014

British Library Cataloguing in Publication Data
Data available

978-1-4085-2013-0

4

Printed in Great Britain

Acknowledgements

Cover photograph: aaM Photography, Ltd/iStockphoto
Illustrations: Andy Keylock
Page make-up: Hart McLeod Ltd, Cambridge

Contents

How to use this book

Transition

The activities and guidance here are to help you bridge the gap between GCSE and AS. There may be particular areas where you are still not confident or where you wish to revise. Look through this at the start of your course and decide what you need to practise. You can always refer back later in the year.

Order of topics

This book is divided into four sections, each of which corresponds to a topic in the Oxford University Press AQA Spanish AS course. While practice activities use simple vocabulary from various subject areas, grammar points are covered in the same order as in the Student Book. This is to help you practise as you go along, reinforcing what you have learned in the classroom with further activities at home.

Mixed practice

At the end of each section there are some mixed practice activities covering the different points you have encountered. You can try these throughout the year or use them for revision while you prepare for your listening, reading and writing exam.

Test yourself

These activities follow a format you are more likely to encounter in the listening, reading and writing paper – hence the rubrics are in Spanish. When you are in the exam you will not be told which grammar points you need to practise, or that a question is particularly geared towards testing your grammar knowledge and accuracy. Therefore it is important to get used to tackling this type of question with confidence.

Longer activities

Some activities will require more extended responses or offer the opportunity for more creative work. For these it will be suggested that you work on a separate sheet of paper. Alternatively you can type up and save your answers to refer to again when revising.

Receptive knowledge only

The AQA specification, which you can consult online, includes a list of the grammatical structures you will be expected to have studied. Some structures are marked with an (R), which indicates receptive knowledge only is required. This means you need to understand phrases and sentences which use the structures but will not need to apply them in your own written and spoken work. Even so, if you are confident in using them yourself you should do so!

Gramática

These offer extra support in understanding the point being tested. Don't refer to them unless you need to! If you need additional information, go to the grammar reference section of your Student Book.

Consejo

These offer extra 'handy hints' for tackling different questions, remembering particular rules and applying your grammar knowledge in practice.

Gramática

Nouns are words that refer to an object or thing, often preceded by 'the' or 'a'.

In Spanish, nouns are always either masculine or feminine. Almost all masculine nouns end in -o, whilst most feminine nouns end in -a, e.g. *el amigo / la amiga, el puerto / la puerta.*

But there are some exceptions:

Masculine word patterns

- words ending in -ma (yes, ma is masculine in Spanish!), e.g. *el programa.*
- **usually** words ending in -e, e.g. *el puente* (exceptions include *la gente, la leche, la calle, la carne*)
- **usually** words ending in -i, -l, -r or -u, e.g. *el autor*

Feminine word patterns

- words ending in -dad (yes, dad is feminine in Spanish!), e.g. *la calidad*
- words ending in -ión and -sis, e.g. *la crisis*

1 Classify the following words into the masculine (el) or feminine (la) categories in the table below.

sistema	calle	ciudad	problema
chico	cuestión	música	publicidad
traje	móvil	argumento	ausencia
televisión	motor	ordenador	

Masculine	Feminine

2 Write el or la before each noun according to whether it is masculine or feminine.

1 ______ tema
2 ______ prioridad
3 ______ mente
4 ______ muerte
5 ______ mapa
6 ______ coche
7 ______ estación
8 ______ planeta
9 ______ yogur
10 ______ cuadro
11 ______ lámpara
12 ______ nación

Gramática

Adjectives are words that add further description to a noun.

The important thing to remember with adjectives is that they must **always** agree with the noun that they are describing. So, if the noun is masculine, so is the adjective. If the noun is plural, then the adjective must also be plural.

The table below shows how standard adjective endings change according to whether they are masculine, feminine, singular or plural.

Masculine form	Feminine form	Masculine plural	Feminine plural
-o	-a	-os	-as
-a	-a	-as	-as
-or *(except comparatives*)*	-ora	-ores	-oras
-án / -ín / -ón	-ana / -ina / -ona *(no accents!)*	-anes / -ines / -ones *(no accents!)*	-anas / -inas / -onas *(no accents!)*
-e	*NO CHANGE*	-es	
consonant	*NO CHANGE*	-es *NOTE:* z ⟶ ces	

*Comparatives such as *mejor* (better), *mayor* (bigger / older), *peor* (worse) and *menor* (less / younger) do not agree with the noun they are describing in gender, but do agree in number, e.g. *Son los **mejores** artículos*. Note that these comparatives go **before** the noun.

1 **Add the appropriate ending on to each adjective, making it agree with the noun it is describing.**

1 (*broken* = roto) la televisión ______________________

2 (*fascinating* = fascinante) la emisión ______________________

3 (*worse* = peor) los resultados ______________________

4 (*unforgettable* = inolvidable) las películas ______________________

5 (*playful* = juguetón) los gatitos ______________________

2 **Convert the following examples into the plural.**

1 el león feroz ______________________

2 el lugar precioso ______________________

3 la palabra incomprensible ______________________

4 la estudiante trabajadora ______________________

5 el jugador actual ______________________

Definite articles – 'the'

Masculine singular	Feminine singular	Masculine plural	Feminine plural
el	la	los	las

Indefinite articles – 'a' / 'an' / 'some'

Masculine singular	Feminine singular	Masculine plural	Feminine plural
un	una	unos	unas

Gramática

Definite articles describe a specific item or thing ('the').

Indefinite articles describe a general item ('a', 'an' or 'some').

Consejo

When talking about professions or nationality, you **do not** include the article, e.g. *Mi madre es enfermera. Soy escocés.* However, you **do** need the article if you include an adjective: *Es **un** cantante famoso.*

1 Choose the correct answer from the options below.

1 *the teachers (female)* ☐
- a los profesores
- b las profesoras
- c unas profesoras

2 *a castle* ☐
- a un castillo
- b el castillo
- c unos castillos

3 *the people* ☐
- a las gente
- b los gente
- c la gente

4 *a city* ☐
- a una ciudad
- b la ciudad
- c el ciudad

5 *some TVs* ☐
- a los televisiones
- b las televisiones
- c unas televisiones

6 *a law* ☐
- a un ley
- b una ley
- c el ley

2 Use the correct definite or indefinite article, if necessary, to complete the following translations.

1 *I like Spanish people.* Me gustan ______ españoles.

2 *I want to be a teacher.* Quiero ser ______ profesora.

3 *I'm interested in water sports.* Me interesan ________ deportes acuáticos.

4 *Music causes aggression.* ______ música provoca agresión.

5 *There are some quite serious problems.* Hay ______ problemas bastante graves.

6 *His father is German.* Su padre es ______ alemán.

7 *I saw a horror film.* Vi ______ película de terror.

8 *Do you fancy going to the pool?* ¿Te apetece ir a ______ piscina?

Gramática

Adjectives are normally placed **after** the noun. However, there are some exceptions: all of the following are placed **before** the noun.

If the noun is masculine singular and comes directly after the adjective, use the shortened form, e.g. *algún chico.*

Masculine singular	Feminine singular	Masculine plural	Feminine plural	Meaning
algún / alguno	alguna	algunos	algunas	*some*
ningún / ninguno	ninguna	*NO PLURAL FORM*		*no / none / neither*
primer / primero	primera	primeros	primeras	*first*
tercer / tercero	tercera	terceros	terceras	*third*

Adjective	Before the noun	After the noun
antiguo	former	old / ancient
gran / grande	great	big
mismo	same	itself (the situation *itself*)
pobre	poor (pitiable)	poor (financial)

Gramática

Some very commonly used adjectives often precede the noun, e.g. *buen / bueno, mal / malo, joven, viejo.*

Remember! There are certain adjectives whose meanings are changed according to where they are positioned (see table opposite).

1 Reorder the words below to create meaningful sentences.

1 *I want to buy a big TV soon.*
comprar quiero televisión una grande pronto

____

2 *I need to watch the first race this afternoon.*
primera carrera tarde ver la esta necesito

____

3 *It's a very dark film with lots of extreme violence.*
película violencia con mucha es una oscura extrema muy

____

4 *In the future I would like to be a great sportsman.*
me ser futuro el deportista gran en gustaría un

____

5 *There are some horrible boys in my class.*
algunos horribles chicos clase mi en hay

____

6 *The former boss of the company announced it yesterday.*
jefe ayer lo la compañía antiguo anunció el de

____

7 *He is from quite a poor family.*
pobre bastante familia una de es

____

8 *Nobody has considered the manufacturers themselves.*
fabricantes mismos ha considerado nadie los a

____

9 *The first time I saw something incredible.*
vi increíble primera la vez algo

____

10 *I want to buy this old chair.*
comprar esta quiero antigua silla

____

11 *There are some obvious examples.*
evidentes ejemplos algunos hay

____

12 *She has the same problems as we do.*
tiene mismos nosotros que problemas los

____

Gramática

The **preterite tense** is used to describe a past, finished event.
It is often translated as '-ed' in English, e.g. I walked, he painted, we visited.
It is formed as follows:
Step 1) Remove the *-ar* / *-er* / *-ir* from the infinitive.
Step 2) Add the following endings according to who did the action.

	-ar	-er	-ir
I (*yo*)	-é	-í	-í
he (*él*) / she (*ella*) / you [formal] (*usted*)	-ó	-ió	-ió
Examples	hablé / habló	bebí / bebió	escribí / escribió

Consejo

The infinitive is the basic form of a verb, which in English is translated as 'to...', e.g. to play, to think. In Spanish there are three types of infinitive: those that end in *-ar*, those that end in *-er* and those that end in *-ir*. All of the verb tenses rely on you knowing your infinitives.

In English there are no patterns to infinitives except that they start with 'to'; this can make English grammar really tricky!

1 **Tick the correct option to translate the verbs in the preterite. Use the advice above, your existing knowledge and common sense!**

1 *I ate* (*comer*)
- **a** comiste ☐
- **b** comí ☐
- **c** comió ☐

2 *She accepted* (*aceptar*)
- **a** acepté ☐
- **b** aceptamos ☐
- **c** aceptó ☐

3 *I described* (*describir*)
- **a** describieron ☐
- **b** describí ☐
- **c** describió ☐

4 *It caused* (*causar*)
- **a** causé ☐
- **b** causasteis ☐
- **c** causó ☐

5 *You [formal] decided* (*decidir*)
- **a** decidiste ☐
- **b** decidí ☐
- **c** decidió ☐

Infinitive	I	He / she / it / you (formal)
decir (*to say*)	dije	dijo
hacer (*to do / make*)	hice	hizo
ir (*to go*)	fui	fue
querer (*to want*)	quise	quiso
ser (*to be*)	fui	fue
tener (*to have*)	tuve	tuvo
ver (*to see*)	vi	vio

Gramática

The table to the left shows some key **irregular preterites**. Notice they do not have written accents.

Remember that compound verbs (which include these infinitives) are also irregular, e.g. ***contener*** (to contain).

2 **Translate the clues to complete the crossword below. Verbs that are irregular in the preterite are marked with an asterisk.**

Down
1. it depended (*depender*)
3. I confirmed (*confirmar*)
4. I broke (*romper*)
6. it allowed (*permitir*)
7. I wrote (*escribir*)
9. she wanted (*querer**)
10. he did (*hacer**)
12. it surprised (*sorprender*)
13. she was unaware (*ignorar*)
16. I danced (*bailar*)
18. it was (*ser**)

Across
2. she answered (*contestar*)
5. she said (*decir**)
8. she learned (*aprender*)
11. I assumed (*asumir*)
13. she interrupted (*interrumpir*)
14. he had (*tener**)
15. he celebrated (*celebrar*)
17. I saw (*ver**)
18. I went (*ir**)

* indicates an irregular preterite

Gramática

The **imperfect tense** is used to describe an ongoing or habitual action in the past – so there's no 'perfect finish'!

It is usually translated as 'was (doing)' or 'used to (do)' in English.

It is formed as follows:

Step 1) Remove the *-ar* / *-er* / *-ir* from the infinitive.

Step 2) Add the following endings according to who did the action.

	-ar	-er	-ir
I (*yo*)	-aba	-ía	-ía
he (*él*) / she (*ella*) / you [formal] (*usted*)	-aba	-ía	-ía
Examples	escuchaba a mi madre	comía mucho pan	vivía en Francia

Gramática

Only three verbs are irregular in the imperfect:

Infinitive	I	he / she / it / you (formal)
ir (*to go*)	iba	iba
ser (*to be*)	era	era
ver (*to see*)	veía	veía

Consejo

Yes, you are right: the 'I' form is **always** exactly the same as the 'he / she / it / you (formal)' form of the imperfect tense.

1a **Decide if the statements below are true or false.**

1b **Correct the false statements on the lines below.**

1 The imperfect tense refers to events in the future. **T / F**

2 To form the imperfect, add the appropriate ending on to the infinitive. **T / F**

3 The imperfect tense means 'was (doing)' or 'used to (do)'. **T / F**

4 To say 'I was' or 'I used to', for an *-ar* verb the ending is *-ía*. **T / F**

5 The endings for 'I' are the same as for 'he / she / it / you (formal)'. **T / F**

6 There are only three irregulars in the imperfect: *ir, ser* and *tener*. **T / F**

Number	Correction?
1	
2	
3	
4	
5	
6	

Gramática

The **conditional tense** refers to something that **would** happen in the future. It is dependent on something else happening first, e.g. *If I spoke perfect Spanish I would…*

To form it, add the following endings according to who did the action on to the end of the infinitive.

	-ar	**-er**	**-ir**
I (*yo*)	-ía	-ía	-ía
he (*él*) / she (*ella*) / you [formal] (*usted*)	-ía	-ía	-ía

Consejo

Point to remember: the 'I' form is **always** exactly the same as the 'he / she / it / you (formal)' form of the conditional tense.

And yes, you are right: the two forms also use the same ending as *-er/ -ir* in the imperfect, but this time the endings come **after** the infinitive.

Irregular conditionals – the key ones!

Infinitive	**I**	**he / she / it / you (formal)**
decir (*to say*)	diría	diría
hacer (*to do / make*)	haría	haría
poder (*to be able to*)	podría	podría
querer (*to want*)	querría	querría
tener (*to have*)	tendría	tendría

1a Circle the five conditional tense verbs in the sentences below.

1b Underline the three verbs that are not in the conditional tense.

1c Write the infinitive (*-ar / -er / -ir*) on the line at the end of each sentence.

1 Me gustaría ver la final mañana. ________

2 Sería fenomenal ir a la playa este fin de semana. ________

3 Tenía que comprar un juego nuevo. ________

4 Comí mucha comida típica. ________

5 Se debería hacer mucho más. ________

6 Visitaría el museo de arte moderno en Madrid. ________

7 No hago caso de la publicidad. ________

8 Volvería al instituto para continuar los estudios. ________

1d Now convert the three non-conditional tense verbs into the conditional tense.

1 ________________________________

2 ________________________________

3 ________________________________

Gramática

The **immediate future tense** is used in Spanish to say 'going to (do)'.

It is formed as follows:

Step 1) Take the appropriate part of the verb *ir* (to go). **Step 2)** Follow it with *a*. **Step 3)** Add an infinitive.

e.g. *Voy a visitar a mi tío, vamos a bañarnos en el mar.*

ir = *to go*	
I (*yo*)	voy
you (*tú*)	vas
he (*él*)	va
she (*ella*)	va
you [formal] (*usted*)	va
we (*nosotros*)	vamos
you [plural] (*vosotros*)	vais
they [masculine] (*ellos*) / they [feminine] (*ellas*) / you [plural, formal] (*ustedes*)	van

1 **Match the Spanish on the left to the English translations on the right.**

1 Vamos a ir a la playa esta tarde.		a *I'm going to buy it.*
2 ¿Vas a ver la película este fin de semana?		b *Are you going to go to the concert tomorrow?*
3 ¿Vais a ir al concierto mañana?		c *It's going to be quite difficult for them.*
4 Pronto van a lanzar otro disco.		d *I'm going to relax a bit.*
5 Voy a comprarlo.		e *They're going to launch a new album soon.*
6 Vamos a tener un problema grande.		f *We're going to go to the beach this afternoon.*
7 Va a ser bastante difícil para ellos.		g *Are you going to see the film this weekend?*
8 Voy a descansar un poco.		h *We're going to have a big problem.*

2a **Find the eight examples of the immediate future in the wordsearch below.**

2b **Translate each example.**

s	p	b	r	q	p	b	r	f	s
v	a	n	a	d	e	c	i	r	o
r	e	e	l	a	y	o	v	r	o
p	c	t	i	s	e	o	g	t	a
v	o	y	a	a	y	u	d	a	r
o	s	u	b	k	y	c	o	e	u
r	e	v	a	s	o	m	a	v	j
v	a	i	s	a	j	u	g	a	r
r	b	v	a	m	o	s	a	i	r
o	k	v	v	a	a	s	e	r	a

	Immediate future	Translation
1		
2		
3		
4		
5		
6		
7		
8		

Gramática

Sentences are made **negative** in Spanish by placing *no* before the verb, e.g. ***no** voy a ir a clase mañana.*

There are other negative words, which add more information.

These words can go before the verb, or stand alone. They can also follow the verb – in this case *no* has to precede the verb so producing a 'double negative', e.g. ***Nadie** está en la clase. ¿Quién está en la clase?* ***No** hay **nadie** en la clase.*

nunca (*more common than* jamás)	never
nada	nothing
nadie	nobody
ningún (*before a masculine singular noun*) / ninguno / ninguna	no (none)
tampoco	nor (opposite of *también*)
ni … ni	neither … nor

1 Choose the correct words from the box in the margin to complete the translation of the sentences.

1 ________ me entiende: normalmente soy bastante tímido.
Nobody understands me: I'm normally quite shy.

2 No hay ________ que hacer – será horrible.
There's nothing that can be done – it will be horrible.

3 No me interesa ________ leer ________ ver la tele – me aburro.
I'm not interested in either reading or watching the TV – I'm bored.

4 ________ quiero ir al parque – está lloviendo.
I don't want to go to the park either – it's raining.

Gramática

Point to remember: *ningunos / ningunas* are only used if the noun does not have a singular form.

e.g. *No veo ningunas gafas en la mesa.*

no	ninguna
ningún	tampoco
nada	ni
nadie	nunca
ni	

2 Reorder the words below to create meaningful sentences, and then on a separate sheet of paper translate them.

1 mejor hay nadie no ________

2 voy piscina nunca la a pequeña ________

3 nada quiero más tampoco no ________

4 fui centro amigos al con mis no ________

5 ningún disco nuevo tengo no ________

Acabo de (*and all parts of* acabar)	I have just …
Al	On …ing
Para	(In order) to
Es importante	It's important to (do)
Tengo que (*and all parts of* tener)	I have to (do)

Gramática

Infinitive constructions are an ideal way to expand your range of expression.

All of the following use the infinitive (the form that ends in *-ar*, *-er* or *-ir*) after them.

3 Use your knowledge of these infinitive constructions and the tenses examined in this Transition section to translate these sentences on a separate sheet of paper. The verbs you need are in the box below.

to work = *trabajar*	to learn = *aprender*	to study = *estudiar*
to pay attention = *prestar atención*	to improve = *mejorar*	to develop = *desarrollar*
to decide = *decidir*	to start = *empezar*	

1 It is going to be important to study more.

2 In order to improve my marks I have to pay attention.

3 I have just read a book in Spanish and I have improved my vocabulary!

4 On starting the course [*el curso*] I decided to study the grammar well.

Topic 1: *Gustar*

Gramática

Gustar means 'to please'. In order to express what you like in Spanish, you use the verb *gustar*, but you have to say **what** it is that pleases, and **whom** it pleases, e.g.

I like ice cream = Ice cream pleases me – *Me gusta el helado.*

He likes swimming = To swim pleases him – *Le gusta nadar.*

	Literal meaning	Accurate translation
Me gusta	It pleases me	I like
Me encanta	It delights me	I love
Me duele	It is hurting to me	It hurts

1 **Choose the correct indirect object pronoun for each example below.**

1 to us ________
2 to them ________
3 to her ________
4 to you (plural) ________
5 to me ________
6 to you (singular) ________
7 to him ________
8 to you (plural, formal) ________

2 **Draw lines to match the English and Spanish sentences, ensuring that you check both the indirect object pronoun and the verb itself.**

1 ¿Te interesaría?	a *I've got three bottles left over.*
2 Me sobran tres botellas.	b *I lacked the necessary patience.*
3 Nos quedaron unos minutos.	c *Would you be interested?*
4 Me faltó la paciencia necesaria.	d *They needed a bit of help.*
5 Les hizo falta un poco de ayuda.	e *We had a few minutes left.*

3 **Translate the sentences below. Think carefully about what tense is being used.**

1 Me sobran diez. ________
2 Te interesó mucho. ________
3 Les interesaría saber un poco más. ________
4 I like them. ________
5 We have got some biscuits left over. ________
6 She used to love it. ________
7 They are hurting me. ________
8 I liked it. ________

Gramática

Gustar, like the verbs below, follows its normal conjugation pattern to say **what** is pleasing and **when** (i.e. what tense), e.g. *gustan* = they are pleasing.

Who is being pleased/interested etc. is indicated by the 'indirect object pronoun' (see page 31).

me = to me
te = to you
le = to him / her / it / you (formal)
nos = to us
os = to you (plural)
les = to them / you (plural, formal)

Similar verbs

interesar – to be interested
faltar – to lack / be missing
hacer falta – to need
sobrar – to have left over / too much of
quedar – to have remaining

Examples:

Le *gustas* = To him you are pleasing (= He likes you)

Nos *quedan dos entradas.* = To us two tickets are remaining. (= We've got two tickets left.)

1 Explain the reason why *por* or *para* has been used in each of the following sentences using numbers 1 to 10 as in the list on the right.

1 Esta casa es perfecta para una familia grande.

____

2 Tengo algunas ideas para mejorar la situación pero no sé qué hacer primero.

____

3 Lo hice por gusto, no por deber.

____

4 Andaba por la calle en el centro.

____

5 Por esta razón no se va a cambiar nada.

____

6 Viajaba por Francia con una amiga para luego visitar a mis abuelos en España.

____

7 Este libro es para ti para celebrar tu cumpleaños.

____

8 No es para nada que fui al gimnasio.

____

2 Choose whether to use *por* or *para* in each case. Cross out the incorrect answer.

1 Gracias **por / para** invitarme a la boda.

2 Pagamos 50 euros **por / para** persona **por / para** comprarlo.

3 **Por / Para** mí será esencial establecer unas normas **por / para** el grupo.

4 Nadar como mínimo dos veces **por / para** semana es bueno **por / para** la salud.

5 Van **por / para** Madrid antes de llegar a su destino en Sevilla.

6 **Por / Para** ganar hace falta tener una actitud egoísta.

3 On a separate sheet of paper, write yourself an explanation of the differences between *por* and *para*. Can you create a story, rhyme or song to help you remember the rules?

Gramática

***Por* or *para*: the great debate!**

There are two ways to say 'for' in Spanish: *por* and *para*. There are specific rules to help you know when to use each word.

Por is used to express causes, reasons, duration and exchange:

1 **Out of / due to**: *Lo hago por interés* (I do it out of interest)

2 **By**: *Estaba motivado por deseo* (he was motivated by desire) / *Fue por mar* (he went by sea)

3 **Through (movement)**: *Viajé por Argentina* (I travelled through Argentina)

4 **Duration of time (similar to *durante*)**: *Fui por dos semanas* (I went for two weeks)

Note also *por la noche* (at / during the night)

5 **Per**: *dos veces por semana* (twice per week)

6 **For**: *Gracias por el regalo* (Thanks for the present)

Para is used to express 'in order to' or 'for' (somebody or something), the idea of futurity or purpose:

7 **Purpose / intention / for (somebody or something)**: *Es para Juan* (It's for Juan)

8 **In order to (+ infinitive)**: *Quiere ir para escuchar al grupo* (She wants to go in order to listen to the band)

9 **Movement towards a direction**: *Voy para Barcelona* (I'm going to [towards] Barcelona)

10 **Achieving a goal / meeting a deadline**: *Lo voy a terminar para el martes* (I'm going to do it by / for Tuesday)

Topic 1: Standard Spanish endings

Gramática

It is easy to expand your knowledge of vocabulary by knowing **standard endings** in Spanish.

- You can guess / work out new words easily.
- You can then skip between types of endings very easily.

For example: automatic = *automático*

automatically = *automáticamente* (note that in this case – that of an adverb – it is the feminine form that is used to create the new word)

English ending	Spanish ending
-ity	-dad (*necesidad*)
-ance	-ancia (*abundancia*)
-ence	-encia (*excelencia*)
-ary	-ario (*aniversario*)
-ous	-oso (*delicioso*)
-ly	-mente (*rápidamente*)
-ic	*-ico* (*Atlántico*) (accent on vowel before ending)
-ical	*-ico* (*clásico*) (accent on vowel before ending)
-ment	-mento (*argumento*)
-y	-ia (*democracia*)
-tion	-ción (*acción*)
-ent	-ente (*agente*)
-ant	-ante (*importante*)

Consejo

Don't forget to use the gender rules from the Transition section (page 5) to put the correct definite article (*el/ la*) or indefinite article (*un / una*) where needed.

Remember that abstract qualities such as 'patience' need the definite article in Spanish. There are two examples in the exercise; can you find them and make sure they have the correct article?

1 **Use the endings rules to write out the Spanish translations of these words.**

1 imagination ____________

2 necessary ____________

3 a situation ____________

4 a community ____________

5 a fanatic ____________

6 electrical ____________

7 a client ____________

8 sarcastic ____________

9 generally ____________

10 a difference ____________

11 a constant ____________

12 tolerance ____________

13 the importance ____________

14 relevant ____________

15 ambitious ____________

Gramática

Comparatives are used to compare things – to say that something is more, less or the same as something else.

más + [adjective / adverb] + *que*
= more [...] than
e.g. *más cuidadosamente que*
= more carefully than

menos + [adjective / adverb] + *que*
= less [...] than
e.g. *menos fácil que*
= less easy than

tan + [adjective / adverb] + *como*
= as [...] as
e.g. *tan rápido como*
= as fast as

Remember: *más / menos* ***de*** = more / less + numbers

e.g. *más de veinte medallas*

= more than 20 medals

tanto / -a / -os / -as + noun = as many ...
– agrees with the noun it is describing
e.g. *Tengo tantos regalos como el año pasado*
= I have as many presents as last year

Superlatives state that something is the best, the worst, the least, the most ... the '-est'!

Formation

el / la / los / las + *más / menos* + adjective

= the most / least + adjective

Irregulars – there are always a few and they are always important!

Adjective	Comparative	Superlative
bueno = good	*mejor* = better	*el mejor* = the best
grande = big	*mayor* = older / greater **Note:** *más grande* = bigger (size)	*el mayor* = the oldest / greatest
malo = bad	*peor* = worse	*el peor* = the worst
pequeño = small	*menor* = younger **Note:** *más pequeño* = smaller (size)	*el menor* = the youngest

1 Insert the necessary word so the Spanish sentences match the English translations.

1 Es mi ________________ amigo. *He's my best friend.*

2 Tiene ________________ suerte que la mayoría. *She has more luck than most people.*

3 Es casi tan perezosa ________________ mi hermana. *She's almost as lazy as my sister.*

4 Hay ________________ gente como en el estadio. *There are as many people as in the stadium.*

5 España ganó menos medallas ________________ durante los últimos Juegos.
Spain won fewer medals than during the last Games.

6 Es ________________ peor de todos los chicos de la clase.
He's the worst of all of the boys in the class.

7 Habrá un poco más ________________ mil personas.
There will be slightly more than one thousand people.

8 Son ________________ asignaturas menos interesantes de todas.
They are the least interesting subjects of them all.

9 Cuando era ________________ de edad el mundo era ________________ .
When I was younger the world was better.

10 ¡Qué va! Las películas de terror son ________________ ridículas como las películas románticas.
Yeah right! Horror films are as ridiculous as romantic films.

Topic 1: *Ser* and *estar*

Gramática

To be and to be, now that is the question!

In Spanish there are two ways to say 'to be': *ser* and *estar*. Using the wrong one can be the difference between being ready (***estar** listo)* or being clever (***ser** listo*) – dramatically different.

Luckily there are set rules to help!

Ser = identity, time, possession, facts and with infinitives or nouns

1 **Identity (usually before a noun or adjective):**
es profesor / inglés / la capital
(he's a teacher / English / it's the capital)
es rojo (it's red)
es guapa (she is beautiful)

2 **Possession:** *es el tuyo* (it's yours)
3 **Time:** *es la una* (it's one o'clock)
4 **Fact:** *es falso* (it's false)
5 **With infinitives:** *leer es relajante* (reading is relaxing)

Estar = location and temporary states (health, mood and ongoing activities)

1 **Location:** *está en España* (he is in Spain)
están de vacaciones en Bilbao (they are on holiday in Bilbao)

Note: To describe where an event will take place in the future, use *ser: Los Juegos serán en España.*

2 **Temporary states:**
estoy de mal humor – I'm in a bad mood
está enferma – she's ill
está viajando – he's travelling
está muy guapa – she's looking very pretty today

1 **Classify the following sentences into the table below according to the reasons why they use *ser* or *estar*.**

1 está aburrido
2 es miércoles
3 estaba haciendo los deberes
4 estaré en casa
5 es muy fácil
6 es evidente
7 es bastante alto
8 están en un restaurante
9 es un restaurante italiano
10 es su coche
11 hablar español es divertido
12 serán las tres y media

Estar		Ser				
Location	Temporary state	Identity	Possession	Time	Fact	With infinitive

2a **Choose the correct verbs – *ser* or *estar* – for each of the following sentences.**

1 Son / Están las tres y media en España.
2 Pepe es / está de mal humor, es / está muy pesado.
3 Era / Estaba ingeniero pero era / estaba aburrido – es / está un trabajo difícil.
4 Soy / Estoy en Buenos Aires: es / está la capital de Argentina y es / está una ciudad preciosa.
5 La respuesta es / está incorrecta – es / está importante revisar lo que has escrito.
6 Deberían ser / estar estudiando y no jugando al fútbol.
7 La mesa es / está de madera y es / está muy barata.
8 Somos / Estamos aficionados a la música heavy, pero según mis padres es / está una fase.

2b **Now translate the sentences on a separate sheet of paper.**

3 **Complete the sentences below with the correct form of *ser* or *estar* to match the English translations.**

1 ___________ alegre. *I am cheerful (by nature).*

2 ___________ en Francia con unos amigos. *I was in France with some friends.*

3 ___________ mi favorito. *It's my favourite.*

4 Sus notas ___________ impresionantes. *Their marks were impressive.*

5 ___________ un poco preocupado – Juan ___________ muy callado ayer.
I am a bit worried – Juan was very quiet yesterday.

6 ___________ muy cansada. *I will be very tired.*

Gramática

The **present tense** is used to talk about the here and now – something ...

- that is happening now.
- that happens on a regular basis.

Formation

Step 1) Remove *-ar* / *-er* / *-ir* from the infinitive.

Step 2) Add the ending for the person who is doing the action.

I	habl**o**	com**o**	viv**o**
you	habl**as**	com**es**	viv**es**
he / she / it / you (formal)	habl**a**	com**e**	viv**e**
we	habl**amos**	com**emos**	viv**imos**
you (plural)	habl**áis**	com**éis**	viv**ís**
they / you (plural, formal)	habl**an**	com**en**	viv**en**

1 Complete the grid below using the regular present tense.

	aprovechar (to make the most of)	***temer*** (to fear)	***decidir*** (to decide)
I			
you			
he / she / it / you (formal)			
we			
you (plural)			
they / you (plural, formal)			

2a Circle the ten verbs in the present tense in the text below (look out for the endings!). Take care: there are two irregular present tense verbs that you should already know.

2b Write the conjugated verb and its infinitive in the table below.

	Conjugated verb	**Infinitive**
1		
2		
3		
4		
5		
6		
7		
8		
9		
10		

Creo que la televisión tiene una influencia negativa en nuestra sociedad. Los niños se levantan y ponen la televisión. No para ver las noticias sino para ver dibujos animados o series estadounidenses. Debemos animar a los jóvenes a llevar una vida más activa – pero es responsabilidad de todos, no sólo de los políticos. En muchos casos estos jóvenes quieren hacer más pero no se les ofrece la oportunidad dado que faltan instalaciones deportivas en su barrio, y por eso no salen para practicar deportes.

2c Use three of these conjugated verbs in sentences of your own.

1 ______________________________

2 ______________________________

3 ______________________________

Topic 1: Irregular present tense verbs

Gramática

There are four types of 'irregular' verb, yet they all follow set patterns.

- Complete irregulars such as *ir* and *ser*
- Irregular 'I' forms
- Radical- or stem-changers, where certain letter patterns are 'different' from normal
- Verbs with spelling changes

Key irregulars

	estar (to be)	*ir* (to go)	*ser* (to be)
I	estoy	voy	soy
you	estás	vas	eres
he / she / it / you (formal)	está	va	es
we	estamos	vamos	somos
you (plural)	estáis	vais	sois
they / you (plural, formal)	están	van	son

Gramática

Irregular 'I' forms

These are regular for all other forms.

The important ones are:

sé – I know (*saber*)

veo – I see (*ver*)

[no accent on *vosotros* form: *veis*]

***-go* verbs**

These are irregular in the 'I' form, and are *-er* / *-ir* verbs only.

The important ones are:

hago – I do / make (*hacer*)

pongo – I put (*poner*)

salgo – I go out (*salir*)

tengo – I have (*tener*)

vengo – I come (*venir*)

Radical- or stem-changers

Tener is also an 'e' to 'ie' radical-changer!

Venir is also an 'i' to 'ie' radical-changer!

We'll look at these verbs on page 39.

Verbs with spelling changes

c to **zc** – irregular in 'I' form only

conducir (to drive)

conduzco – I drive

g to ***j*** – changes take place before an 'a' or 'o'

elijo – I choose (*elegir*)

corrijo – I correct (*corregir*)

Elegir is also an 'e' to 'i' radical-changer (see page 39).

gu to **g** – irregular in 'I' form only

sigo – I follow (*seguir*)

Also *conseguir*, *perseguir*, etc.

Seguir is also an 'e' to 'i' radical-changer (see page 39).

1 **Conjugate the following present tense verbs. Think carefully about which part you are conjugating and whether it is irregular or not.**

1 esperar *they wait* ____________________

2 ver *I see* ____________________

3 tener *we have* ____________________

4 hacer *you (sing.) do* ____________________

5 enviar *they send* ____________________

6 saber *I know* ____________________

7 decidir *we decide* ____________________

8 leer *she reads* ____________________

9 comprar *you (pl. formal) buy* ____________________

10 salir *he goes out* ____________________

Consejo

It is essential that you know the 'I' forms of the present tense. The present subjunctive (see page 33) is based on this form.

Gramática

The **impersonal *se*** is used to describe an action done by 'people in general' or 'you'.

It is formed as follows: *se* + 3rd person singular

e.g. *se puede* = you (people in general) can

se debe = you (people in general) should

The **passive** is used to describe something that has happened to someone or something, but without saying who did it.

In Spanish it is commonly expressed as follows: *se* + 3rd person singular or plural

e.g. *La tortilla se comió.* = Someone ate the tortilla.

Se venden caramelos en la tienda. = Sweets are sold in the shop.

Points to remember:

1 'Impersonal' statements are often followed by an infinitive, e.g. *se debe hacer algo*. Passive statements are usually followed by an object.

2 Take care not to get confused with *se* used as a reflexive pronoun, e.g. *se levanta* = he gets (himself) up. In this case the *se* says that he / she / it is doing the action to themselves!

3 Plurals are **only** used in passive sentences when more than one person or thing is doing the action to the object.

1 **Decide if each of the statements below is 'impersonal' or 'passive' and complete the sentences with the relevant part of the verb.**

Think carefully about the tense and if the verb should be singular or plural.

1 ______________ que los deberes son inútiles. (**opinar**)

2 ______________ apreciar la belleza del paisaje. (**poder**)

3 ______________ aprender algo más sobre el cine latinoamericano. (**deber**)

4 ______________ unos pantalones allí pero son muy feos. (**vender**)

5 Hace veinte años ______________ una vida mucho más sencilla. (**vivir**)

6 ______________ muchos idiomas en este hotel. (**hablar**)

7 Desde hace muchos años ______________ fumar en lugares públicos. (**prohibir**)

8 En mi clase de historia ______________ demasiado. (**escribir**)

9 En el futuro ______________ en coches volantes. (**viajar**)

10 Lamentablemente ______________ sufriendo por los efectos de las toxicomanías. (**seguir**)

2 **Translate the following sentences into Spanish, taking care with your use of the impersonal *se* and passive.**

1 How do you say 'terrified' in Spanish?

____

2 People pay huge fines every year.

____

3 They rent out bikes in the shop near the river.

____

4 You can visit the museum and the cathedral.

____

5 Every afternoon people go to the café to talk about politics.

____

6 In the local college they offer lots of interesting courses for older people.

____

7 In the restaurant next to the station they serve a delicious fish soup.

____

8 I'm sorry, they ate the cake yesterday.

____

Topic 1: *Lo* with an adjective or an adverb

> **Gramática**
>
> There are two different ways to use ***lo*** with an adjective.
>
> 1 *lo* + masculine adjective = the ... thing – focusing on the 'essence' of the adjective
>
> e.g. ***Lo malo** es que no queda mucho tiempo* = **The bad thing** is that there's not much time left.
>
> 2 *lo* + superlative adverb + *posible*
>
> e.g. ***lo más rápidamente** posible* = **the fastest** possible

1 Insert the correct adjective or adverb and any other required words to complete the sentences below, so they match the English translation.

1 Entrenaba lo más duro ________________ .

= *He used to train the hardest possible.*

2 Decidió que lo ________________ sería ignorarlo.

= *He decided that the dangerous thing would be to ignore it.*

3 Lo ________________ era el parque acuático.

= *The amusing thing was the water park.*

4 Lo ________________ es que nadie sabe la verdad.

= *The interesting thing is that nobody knows the truth.*

5 Quiere mejorar lo más ________________

= *She wants to improve as fast as possible.*

6 Lo ________________ del problema es que afecta a mucha gente.

= *The important thing about the problem is that it affects lots of people.*

7 Se debería cambiarlo ________________ .

= *They should change it as soon as possible.*

8 Todos los concursantes quieren hacer lo ________________ .

= *All the competitors want to do the best possible.*

2 Translate the sentences below into English, taking care how you translate the *lo*.

1 Lo peligroso de esta situación es también lo más atractivo.

____

2 Lo preocupante es que nadie me llamó.

____

3 Debes comprar algo lo más rápidamente posible.

____

4 Lo aconsejable sería terminar el trabajo inmediatamente.

____

5 Lo bueno es que no causó mucho daño.

____

6 Siempre conduce lo más eficientemente posible.

____

7 Es lo más feo que he visto en mi vida.

____

8 Lo fundamental es prepararse rigurosamente.

____

Gramática

Disjunctive pronouns are only used after prepositions such as *por*, *para*, *de*, *en* or *a*. They are also known as emphatic pronouns because they emphasise other words.

e.g. *no quiero hablar de **él***

de = preposition = of / about *él* = disjunctive pronoun = him

The disjunctive pronouns are identical to the normal subject pronouns that you learned when you first learned how to form a verb – except in two cases, as shown below: *mí* and *ti*.

Subject pronoun	Disjunctive pronoun	Subject pronoun	Disjunctive pronoun
yo	mí (accent!)	nosotros	nosotros
tú	ti	vosotros	vosotros
él	él	ellos	ellos
ella	ella	ellas	ellas
usted	usted	ustedes	ustedes

1 Match the pronouns a–h with the English sentences 1–8. Are these disjunctive or subject pronouns?

1 I did it for you.
2 Everyone was talking about her.
3 It is crucial for them.
4 According to you *(plural)* all it's a great film.
5 Is that present for me?
6 He came with me.
7 Amongst ourselves it is a big issue.
8 Nobody understands it except me.

a ellos
b vosotros
c ti
d ella
e nosotros
f mí
g yo
h conmigo

Gramática

With the preposition *con* we say *conmigo* (with me), *contigo* (with you), *consigo* (with him(self) / her(self) / you(rself) (formal)). Notice the difference between *Llevó las llaves **consigo*** (they were in his own pocket) and *Fue **con él*** (with another person).

Points to remember:

1 *mí* has an accent to make it different from *mi* meaning 'my'

e.g. *mi libro* = my book

2 Not all prepositions need disjunctive pronouns: *entre*, *según*, *menos*, *excepto* and *salvo* are followed by subject pronouns.

3 *ello* is used when you are talking about an abstract idea, to say 'it'.

2 Insert the correct preposition and disjunctive pronoun in the sentences to match the English translation.

1 No, los compré ________________ . *No, I bought them for you.*

2 Traje algo ________________ también. *I brought something for her as well.*

3 Tengo que ir de vacaciones ________________ . *I've got to go on holiday with them.*

4 Estaba sentado ________________ . *I was sitting next to you (formal).*

5 Fui al concierto ________________ anoche. *I went to the concert with him last night.*

6 Según María hay un regalo ________________ en la oficina.

According to María there's a present for us in the office.

7 Lo arreglaré ________________, pero será bastante caro.

I will sort it out for you (pl. formal) but it will be quite expensive.

8 No estábamos listos ________________ . *We weren't ready for it.*

1 **Write a short sentence in Spanish to compare each of the following things.**

1 Using an iPad to using a laptop ______

2 Watching TV to listening to the radio ______

3 Surfing the internet to reading a book ______

4 Britain to Spain as a holiday destination ______

5 Travelling by plane to travelling by car ______

2 **Complete the Spanish sentences below. Use the grammar items that you have studied in this topic so that they match the English statements.**

1 ____ ______ importante es que la publicidad moderna es ______ interesante.

The most important thing is that modern advertising is more interesting.

2 Lo ______ de ver la tele es que ____ puede pasar ______ tiempo con la familia.

The good thing about watching TV is that you can spend more time with your family.

3 Manuela ______ de un humor muy ______ porque viaja ______ Málaga.

Manuela is in a very bad mood because she's travelling through Málaga.

4 ______ comprar algo ______ Zara ______ su ayuda.

We want to buy something for Zara for her help.

5 ¿ ____ ______ algunos? ______ probar uno.

Have you got any left over? I want to try one.

3 **Write these questions in Spanish. Take care! Think through all of the grammar points that are being tested.**

1 We follow the best advice of the experts. ______

2 The worst thing when I go out with my friends is how much we spend.

______

3 Do you (pl.) like what you (pl.) see?

______

4 We're going to a remote beach – for me it's the most beautiful.

______

5 You shouldn't always buy the most popular or the most expensive products.

______

6 It's a classic programme, but we don't like it at all.

______

7 They are in Barcelona, in one of the cheapest hotels.

______

8 We've got two days left before the most fun night of our lives.

______

1 **Completa esta descripción del mundo de los ordenadores, escogiendo palabras de la lista A–L. Escribe la letra y la palabra en los espacios en blanco. ¡Ojo! No necesitarás todas las palabras.**

El ordenador personal es uno de los iconos de los años ochenta y noventa. Cambió completamente nuestra forma de vivir. No obstante, el mercado ________________ cambiando y parece importante preguntar: ¿el ordenador personal está en su fase terminal?

Ahora se ________________ mucho ________________ de teléfonos inteligentes de nueva generación y también de tabletas – productos más atractivos ________________ los ordenadores tradicionales. En muchos casos se compra una tableta en lugar de una computadora personal ________________ razones prácticas pero también para asociarse con uno de los símbolos de estatus más importantes de nuestra generación. Pero la verdad es que hoy en día nos gusta estar enchufados a cada momento. No se quiere esperar hasta llegar a casa ________________ enviar un email, ni para comparar el precio de un producto en nuestras páginas favoritas – queremos acceder a la información lo antes posible.

Así que la innovación ha llegado a ________________ el pasado. ¿Y el futuro? Pues, a ver …

A	ser
B	habla
C	es
D	por
E	que
F	estar
G	menos
H	para
I	hablar
J	está
K	tan
L	más

Consejo

This is more like the kind of question you will encounter in the exam and is called a cloze test.

Before filling in any answers, read through the text and suggested answers very carefully. Think about what kind of word is needed in each gap: verb, noun, adjective, etc. Then see which words are being suggested. Which one makes sense? If you aren't sure about the meaning of a word, you might be able to work out the word you need by a process of elimination!

2a **Rellena los espacios en las frases siguientes con la forma adecuada de la palabra en paréntesis, utilizando el presente para todos los infinitivos.**

2b **Traduce las frases en una hoja aparte.**

1. Lamentablemente yo no ________________ (poder) ir contigo – ________________ (hacer) mucho deporte cada fin de semana.
2. Mi padre ________________ (utilizar) una tableta moderna pero yo ________________ (seguir) utilizando este ordenador viejo.
3. Normalmente yo ________________ (comprar) productos reciclados pero no se ________________ (vender) muchos en mi pueblo.
4. En mi opinión ________________ (ver) demasiada telebasura pero nos ________________ (encantar).
5. Mi hermano ________________ (estar) en Madrid por trabajo durante casi un mes, pero nuestros primos ________________ (vivir) allí también.

Consejo

When filling in a missing verb, check that you know which tense it is – is it a finite verb or do you need the past participle, infinitive, etc.? If it is a finite verb, does it have the correct ending to go with the subject in the sentence?

Topic 2: Demonstrative adjectives and pronouns

Gramática

Demonstrative adjectives go before a noun to say 'this', 'that', 'these' or 'those'.

They agree with what they are describing – if the noun is feminine, the demonstrative adjective must be feminine etc.

	Masc. sing.	Fem. sing.	Masc. pl.	Fem. pl.
this/these	este	esta	estos	estas
that/those	ese	esa	esos	esas
that/those (over there, further from where you are)	aquel	aquella	aquellos	aquellas

Gramática

Demonstrative pronouns stand in the place of those nouns, i.e. 'this one',' that one', 'these ones' or 'those ones'.

	Masc. sing.	Fem. sing.	Masc. pl.	Fem. pl.
this/these one(s)	éste	ésta	éstos	éstas
that/those one(s)	ése	ésa	ésos	ésas
that/those one(s) (over there, further from where you are)	aquél	aquélla	aquéllos	aquéllas

1 **On a separate sheet of paper, rewrite the sentences below, changing the definite article (*el / la / los / las*) to the correct demonstrative adjective to match the English translations.**

1 El chico sería menos capaz que la chica.
That boy would be less capable than this girl.

2 Los juegos no son tan impresionantes como esperaba.
These games are not as impressive as I had hoped.

3 Odio los anuncios que tratan de los productos innecesarios.
I hate those adverts that are about these unnecessary products.

4 La dieta es importante para mantenerse en forma.
This diet is important for staying in shape.

5 Las fiestas en España son una locura.
Those Spanish festivals are crazy.

Consejo

The accent tells you that it is a pronoun – that it is taking the place of the noun.

Gramática

If you are describing an idea or a feeling, you are not describing something that is either masculine or feminine, so you use a **neuter** pronoun:

esto = this (thing)
eso = that (thing)
aquello = that (thing over there)

Note that these don't have accents.

2 **Fill in the gaps below in order to translate the English paragraph.**

__________ es un problema que no se debe ignorar. __________ noticias recientes sobre el cambio climático son muy graves, y no se puede decir que son "__________" científicos o políticos los que tienen la responsabilidad de solucionar __________ situación. __________ argumento no sirve para nada. __________ es nuestro planeta, ¿pero dónde está nuestro plan?

This is a problem that we should not ignore. These recent news stories about climate change are very serious, and we can't suggest that it is 'those' scientists or politicians who have the responsibility to resolve this situation. That argument doesn't achieve anything. This is our planet, but where is our plan?

Gramática

Read through the Transition section again (page 9) to refresh your memory of the basics of the **preterite tense**.

The preterite tense is used to describe a past, finished event. It is usually translated as '-ed' in English, e.g. I worked, he rested, we listened.

Formation

Step 1) Remove the infinitive ending (*-ar* / *-er* / *-ir*).

Step 2) Add the appropriate ending for who did the action.

Who?	-ar	-er	-ir
I	-é	-í	-í
you	-aste	-iste	-iste
he / she / it / you (formal)	-ó	-ió	-ió
we	-amos	-imos	-imos
you (pl.)	-asteis	-isteis	-isteis
they / you (pl. formal)	-aron	-ieron	-ieron

1 Complete the grid below, inserting the correct conjugated forms of each verb.

Consejo

Remember:

1. *-er* and *-ir* verbs use the same endings in the preterite.
2. Take care with the 'we' form of the *-ar* verbs – it's the same as in the present tense! The context should show you if a verb is in the present or the preterite tense.

apoyar	*to support*	prometer	*to promise*	decidir	*to decide*
	I supported		*I promised*		*I decided*
	you supported		*you promised*		*you decided*
	he / she / you (formal) supported		*he / she / you (formal) promised*		*he / she / you (formal) decided*
	we supported		*we promised*		*we decided*
	you (pl.) supported		*you (pl.) promised*		*you (pl.) decided*
	they / you (pl. formal) supported		*they / you (pl. formal) promised*		*they / you (pl. formal) decided*

2 Find the ten preterite verbs in the word snake. Write them on ten lines, on a separate sheet of paper, and then translate them. Take care, there is one irregular verb hidden in the snake!

Hablaronvolvídescansamostemiópermitisteisfuidefinistedependiólucharoncambié

3 On a separate sheet of paper, write an explanation for yourself of the meaning, usage and formation of the preterite tense.

Record this on your phone as a revision tool for later on – the preterite is a very important thing to learn as it is used a lot in Spanish!

Topic 2: More on the imperfect tense

Gramática

The **imperfect tense was** confusing, **used to be** hard ... but not any more! You read the basics in the Transition section (page 10). It is used to describe:

- What something **was** like, e.g. it was old
- What someone or something **used to** do (in the past)
- What **was** happen**ing** – the narration of a story. This narration is often interrupted by the preterite: 'I **was** play**ing** [imperfect] in the park when my friend call**ed** [preterite]'.

Formation

Step 1) Remove the infinitive ending (*-ar* / *-er* / *-ir*).

Step 2) Add the appropriate ending for who did the action.

Who?	-ar	-er	-ir
I	-aba	-ía	-ía
you	-abas	-ías	-ías
he / she / it / you (formal)	-aba	-ía	-ía
we	-ábamos	-íamos	-íamos
you (pl.)	-abais	-íais	-íais
they / you (pl. formal)	-aban	-ían	-ían

Consejo

Remember:

1. *-er* and *-ir* verbs use the same endings in the imperfect!
2. The only accent on *-ar* verbs is on the 'a' before the 'b' of the *nosotros* form.

1a **Use your knowledge of the imperfect to write the correct infinitive next to the conjugated verb. Think carefully what the ending is telling you!**

1b **Translate the verb, using a dictionary where necessary.**

1. existíamos __________ __________
2. averiguaba __________ __________
3. sucedía __________ __________
4. corrías __________ __________
5. añadían __________ __________
6. aprovechaba __________ __________
7. ocurría __________ __________
8. sorprendías __________ __________
9. jurábamos __________ __________
10. emitían __________ __________

2 **On a separate sheet of paper, write your own explanation of the meaning, usage and formation of the imperfect tense.**

Record this on your phone as a revision tool for later on – the imperfect is a very important thing to learn as it is used a lot in Spanish!

Gramática

The **perfect tense** is used to describe a recently finished event. It is usually translated as 'has ...' / 'have ...' in English, e.g. he has finished.

It is important to distinguish between the perfect and preterite tenses.

The perfect tense is:

- used for more recent events
- used to describe events / actions which are still relevant to something that's happening now, e.g. *He llegado, por fin* = I've arrived, finally
- **less common** than the preterite

Although in English we say 'I have learnt Spanish for four years' (using the perfect tense), in Spanish the present tense is used as it is something we continue to do, in the present: *Aprendo el español desde hace cuatro años.*

Formation

The perfect tense is a 'compound' tense – it has more than one part.

Part 1) *haber* in the present tense (this is known as the auxiliary as it helps the second part of the verb – the past participle)

Part 2) the past participle

Step 1) Remove the infinitive ending (*-ar* / *-er* / *-ir*).

Step 2) Add *-ado* for *-ar* verbs. Add *-ido* for *-er* or *-ir* verbs.

	auxiliary	**past participle**
I have finished	he	terminado
you have finished	has	terminado
he / she / it / you (formal) has / have finished	ha	terminado
we have finished	hemos	terminado
you (pl.) have finished	habéis	terminado
they / you (pl. formal) have finished	han	terminado

1 **On a separate sheet of paper, write the past participles for the infinitives below.**

1 hacer
2 cumplir
3 admitir
4 cubrir
5 luchar
6 volver
7 combatir
8 disuadir
9 permitir

2 **Translate the following verbs using the perfect tense. Remember to use both parts – the auxiliary and the past participle.**

1 I have gone out (*salir*) ____________________
2 We have fought (*luchar*) ____________________
3 You (sing.) have promised (*prometer*) ____________________
4 Have you (pl.) received ...? (*recibir*) ____________________
5 They have opened ... (*abrir*) ____________________
6 She has adopted ... (*adoptar*) ____________________
7 He has died (*morir*) ____________________
8 I've said (*decir*) ____________________

Gramática

Key irregulars

	infinitive	**past participle**
to say	*decir*	*dicho*
to discover	*descubrir*	*descubierto**
to write	*escribir*	*escrito*
to do / make	*hacer*	*hecho*
to go	*ir*	*ido*
to die	*morir*	*muerto*
to break	*romper*	*roto*
to put	*poner*	*puesto*
to see	*ver*	*visto*
to return	*volver*	*vuelto*

Also works with other '-brir*'

3 **On a separate sheet of paper, use the five infinitives below to create a message of no more than 40 characters in the perfect tense, describing what you have (or haven't!) done so far today.**

You could start off like this: *Esta mañana no he ...*

comer ver hacer decidir escuchar

Gramática

The **present continuous** is used to describe an ongoing action that is taking place **right now**. It is usually translated as 'to be -ing'.

Formation

Part 1) the correct part of *estar* (to be)

I am	*estoy*
you are	*estás*
he / she / it is / you (formal) are	*está*
we are	*estamos*
you (pl.) are	*estáis*
they are / you (pl. formal) are	*están*

Part 2) the present participle (also known as the gerund)

Step 1) Remove the infinitive ending (*-ar* / *-er* / *-ir*).

Step 2) *-ar* verbs add *-ando*, e.g. *habl**ando***

-er / *-ir* verbs add *-iendo*, e.g. *com**iendo** / viv**iendo***

Remember:

1 The present participle **does not** change depending on who is doing the action.

2 The present continuous tense is a 'compound tense' as it has two parts, unlike the one-word tenses such as the preterite or imperfect.

Key irregulars

These verbs are irregular in their present participle form because some are radical-changing in the present tense; some follow specific spelling change patterns.

	infinitive	**present participle**
to say	*decir*	*diciendo*
to sleep	*dormir*	*durmiendo*
to read	*leer*	*leyendo*
to ask (for)	*pedir*	*pidiendo*
to be able to	*poder*	*pudiendo*
to follow	*seguir*	*siguiendo*
to come	*venir*	*viniendo*

Points to remember:

1 In English we often say '-ing' at the start of the sentence, e.g. 'Listening to the teacher is important.' In Spanish we **do not** use the present participle form – we use an infinitive! *Es importante escuchar al profesor.*

2 To say that you are still doing something we use the correct part of *continuar* (to continue) + the present participle or *seguir* (to carry on / keep) + the present participle.

e.g. *Sigue estudiando pero sin mucho éxito* = he is still studying (he keeps on studying) but without much success.

3 It is very easy to use continuous tenses in different time frames, e.g. the imperfect continuous uses the imperfect of *estar: estaba comiendo cuando ...*

1 **Write the present participle for each of the infinitives below.**

1 fingir ____________	4 explicar ____________	7 hacer ____________
2 ver ____________	5 proteger ____________	8 intentar ____________
3 decidir ____________	6 investigar ____________	9 seguir ____________

2 **Provide appropriate translations for the sentences below, thinking carefully about whether to use *estar*, *seguir*, *continuar* or an infinitive construction.**

1 I am trying to explain the main problems.

____

2 They are having a coffee in the town centre.

____

3 We like going to see matches regularly.

____

4 He keeps interrupting me.

____

5 Are you practising enough? [Note: enough = *lo suficiente* in this context]

____

6 She is improving but she must keep studying.

____

Gramática

Direct object (DO) pronouns

Whatever (person or thing) receives the action of a verb is called the 'direct object', e.g. he watches **the match**.

A direct object pronoun replaces the noun that the verb is referring to, e.g. he watches **it**.

An indirect object pronoun again replaces a noun – this time in order to say 'to someone', e.g. 'to me', 'to him / her', e.g. he gives the match programme **to her**.

me	*me*	us	*nos*
you	*te*	you (pl.)	*os*
him / it	*lo / le*	them (masc.)	*los / les*
her / it	*la*	them (fem.)	*las*
you (formal)	*lo / le*	you (pl. formal)	*les*

Gramática

It usually goes **before** a verb, e.g. *¿Me quieres?* (Do you love me?)

But when used with the following constructions it goes on the end:

1 a gerund, e.g. *estoy comiéndo**lo***
2 an infinitive, e.g. *no quiero comer**lo***
3 a positive command, e.g. *escúcha**me***

Indirect object (IDO) pronouns

There are only two forms which are different from direct object pronouns:

le (to him / her / you [formal]) **instead of** *le / la / lo*

les (to them / you [pl. formal]) **instead of** *les / las / los*

Word order

An indirect object pronoun is always used before the direct object pronoun – unlike in English.

e.g. *¿Me **lo** enviaste ayer?* – Did you send **it** to me yesterday?

IDO **DO** **DO** IDO

But if the IDO *le / les* is followed by the DO *lo, le, la, los, les* or *las* the IDO changes into *se*.

e.g. *se lo dimos* = we gave it to her

If there is still ambiguity (who is it being given to precisely?), use a disjunctive pronoun to clarify matters.

e.g. *se lo dimos a ella*

1 **Match the sentences (1–6) with their appropriate responses (a–f) and insert the correct object pronouns.**

1 ¿Por qué no nos saludasteis ayer? ☐
2 ¿Te has acordado de dar a José su regalo? ☐
3 ¿Qué opinas de las películas de Almodóvar? ☐
4 ¿Sabes que Cristina volvió esta mañana? ☐
5 ¿Dónde aprendiste castellano? ☐
6 ¿Vais a la boda de Simón y Sofía? ☐

a Sí – todavía no _____ he llamado pero quiero ver_____ pronto.
b Claro, _____ _____ di ayer.
c Lamentablemente no _____ invitaron, pero _____ voy a enviar algo.
d Porque no _____ vimos – no hay otra razón, _____ _____ prometo.
e Mi vecino _____ _____ enseñó – es argentino.
f _____ encantan, pero creo que tiene una imaginación rarísima.

Consejo

When you add a syllable to a word, e.g. in the form of a pronoun, a written accent is often needed to maintain the stress pattern of the original word, e.g. *escucha* (stress on penultimate syllable 'u'), *escúchame* (written accent needed to show where the original stress fell).

Consejo

You cannot ever say ...
le lo
le la

Commit facts like these to memory!

Gramática

We have no equivalent to the **personal 'a'** in English. It is needed in Spanish when the direct object of the verb is a person, and is placed between the verb and the name of the person.

'A' as a preposition is usually translated as 'to' in English, but in the case of the personal '*a*' usually it does not need translating.

e.g. *veo mucho **a** Juanita* *tengo que pasear **al** perro*

We use the personal '*a*' before:

- Human direct objects: *Quiero convencer **a** Marta.*
- Pronouns representing a person (*alguien, nadie, usted*, etc): *Vi **a** Marta con su novio la semana pasada.*
- Known animals: *Busco **a** mi tortuga, Harriet – se ha escapado.*
- Collective nouns referring to groups of people such as countries, teams, etc.: *Nadie va a convencer **a** la gente.*

However, the personal 'a' is generally **not** used:

1 after *tener* e.g. *tengo una hija y dos hijos*

except if you are holding someone / have someone there with you

e.g. *tengo a mi esposa en los brazos / tenemos a un experto aquí con nosotros*

2 **unless** you are talking about a specific person rather than a person in general from a group

e.g. *Quiero ver un payaso* = I want to see a clown (any clown, not a specific clown)

*Quiero ver **a** un payaso que se llama Manolo* = I want to see a clown called Manolo

1 **Choose the correct option in each case.**

1 **a** Conozco Barcelona muy bien. ☐
b Conozco a Barcelona muy bien. ☐

2 **a** No quiero visitar a mi abuela este fin de semana. ☐
b No quiero visitar mi abuela este fin de semana. ☐

3 **a** Quiero ver a *La Oreja de Van Gogh* en concierto. ☐
b Quiero ver *La Oreja de Van Gogh* en concierto. ☐

4 **a** Dejaron Juan fuera del equipo. ☐
b Dejaron a Juan fuera del equipo. ☐

5 **a** Pronto van a prohibir la publicidad del tabaco. ☐
b Pronto van a prohibir a la publicidad del tabaco. ☐

2 **Complete the sentences below, inserting the personal '*a*' where appropriate.**

1 No conozco ____ nadie que sepa tocar la guitarra.
2 Voy al parque con ____ mis amigos.
3 Sí, Juanma pegó ____ Pepe fuera de la discoteca.
4 Necesito ____ un fontanero que trabaje los fines de semana.
5 ¿Recuerdas ____ la película de que me hablaste? La vi y no la recomendaría ____ nadie.

Consejo

Notice the phrase *nadie que sepa* in Question 1 of Exercise 2. The verb is in the subjunctive mood (*sepa* instead of *sabe*) because it's unclear who this person might be who knows how to play the guitar. There is more about the subjunctive on pages 33–34.

3 **On a separate sheet of paper, translate the sentences below, focusing on your use of the personal '*a*'.**

1 I am looking for someone to share a flat [*compartir piso*].
2 We have eight cats and three dogs.
3 I didn't see anyone yesterday, I had to work.
4 This summer I want to go on holiday with my family.
5 I need something a bit more complicated.
6 Last night I met the girl of my dreams.

Gramática

The **subjunctive** is a mood not a tense – it's an important difference!

The tenses that you have studied so far (the present, the preterite, etc.) all refer to definite actions – they are known as indicative because they indicate something 'real'.

The subjunctive is different. It's not as certain. It might happen. You don't think that it'll happen. You fear it might happen.

The subjunctive is easy to form and follows strict rules, so when you know those it's simple to use. We'll look at the formation first, which is easy when you know the present tense.

Formation

Step 1) Remove the infinitive ending (*-ar* / *-er* / *-ir*).

Step 2) Add the appropriate endings.

Regular subjunctives

	-ar	**-er**	**-ir**
	hablar (*to speak*)	**beber (*to drink*)**	**vivir (*to live*)**
I	habl**e**	beb**a**	viv**a**
you	habl**es**	beb**as**	viv**as**
he / she / it / you (formal)	habl**e**	beb**a**	viv**a**
we	habl**emos**	beb**amos**	viv**amos**
you (pl.)	habl**éis**	beb**áis**	viv**áis**
they / you (pl. formal)	habl**en**	beb**an**	viv**an**

Consejo

Make sure you know how to form the present tense before you tackle the present subjunctive!

Check that you can remember what the following terms mean and how they're formed in the present tense.

- regular endings
- irregular 'I' forms

An easy way to remember how to form the present subjunctive is to 'swap over' the present tense endings: the *-ar* subjunctive uses the *-er* present tense endings, whilst the *-er* and *-ir* present subjunctives are formed using the endings of the present tense *-ar* verbs!

Gramática

Key irregulars

1 Using the irregular stems provided by the 'I' form in the present tense to create the subjunctive stem

	infinitive	**present subjunctive**
to say	*decir*	*diga* etc.
to do / make	*hacer*	*haga* etc.
to be able to	*poder*	*pueda* etc.
to want	*querer*	*quiera* etc.
to have	*tener*	*tenga* etc.
to go out	*salir*	*salga* etc.
to come	*venir*	*venga* etc.
to put	*poner*	*ponga* etc.

2 Complete irregulars – but they still use the regular present subjunctive endings!

	infinitive	**present subjunctive**
to have*	*haber*	*haya* etc.
to go	*ir*	*vaya* etc.
to know	*saber*	*sepa* etc.
to be	*ser*	*sea* etc.

*the subjunctive form of *hay* (there is)

1 Put the verbs provided into the correct form of the subjunctive as indicated in brackets.

	infinitive	**'I' form of present indicative**	**present subjunctive**
1	cambiar	cambio	(yo) ______
2	tener	tengo	(tú) ______
3	admitir	admito	(nosotros) ______
4	poder	puedo	(usted) ______
5	dormir	duermo	(él) ______

Topic 2: When to use the subjunctive

1a Complete the sentences below using the verbs provided.

1b Indicate whether each sentence needs a subjunctive or not.

1 No creo que mucha gente ________________ cambiar la situación. (**querer, ella**)

SUBJ / NO SUBJ

2 Cuando ________________ mayores tendréis que esforzaros un poco más. (**ser, vosotros**)

SUBJ / NO SUBJ

3 Es posible que ________________ problemas graves a causa de la sequía reciente. (**haber, ellos**)

SUBJ / NO SUBJ

4 Espero ________________ ir, pero depende de mis padres. (**poder, yo**)

SUBJ / NO SUBJ

5 Recomiendo que ________________ su nuevo disco. (**comprar, tú**)

SUBJ / NO SUBJ

6 Es mejor que lo ________________ . (**olvidar, tú**)

SUBJ / NO SUBJ

7 Temo que ________________ algo más profundo. (**esconder, ellas**)

SUBJ / NO SUBJ

8 Para mejorar, es importante ________________ cada día. (**practicar**)

SUBJ / NO SUBJ

9 ¡Que ________________ un buen día! (**tener, tú**)

SUBJ / NO SUBJ

10 Creo que el flamenco ________________ muy emocionante. (**ser**)

SUBJ / NO SUBJ

Gramática

The **subjunctive** is used for:

W wishes, desires – *quiero que, espero que, insisto en que, que ...*

E emotion – *me sorprende que, me alegro de que*

I impersonals – *es importante que, es posible que*

R recommendations – *recomiendo que, sugiero que*

D doubt / denial / disbelief – *no creo que*, dudo que, no pienso que, niego que, tal vez*

O *ojalá que* ('if only...')

*The subjunctive **can** be used in a questioning state of disbelief, e.g. *¿En serio, crees que* ***vaya*** *a llover?*

The subjunctive can also be used for:

- *cuando* + reference to a future event / action

The subjunctive can be tricky because we don't feel like it exists in English. It does, we're just not aware of it!

e.g. 'God bless you' ('May God might bless you'), 'I wish I were richer'

The subjunctive can only be used if the subject of the subjunctive is different to that of an introductory verb.

e.g.	*quiero*	*comer* NO SUBJUNCTIVE
	subject = I	subject = I
	quiero que	*coman* SUBJUNCTIVE
	subject = I	subject = they

Gramática

Ser and ***estar*** both mean 'to be'. On page 18 we learned that:

ser = used for identity (*es inglés*), time (*son las tres*), facts (*es verdad*), and with infinitives / nouns (*es un perro*).

estar = used for location (*estoy en Sevilla*) and temporary states, health (*estoy enfermo*), mood (*estoy enfadado*) and ongoing activities (*estoy descansando*).

However, there are times when *ser* and *estar* can be used with the same adjective to mean something completely different from each other. Get them mixed up and you can get completely the wrong end of the stick!

adjective	with *ser*	with *estar*
aburrido	boring	bored
bueno	good person	tastes good / is attractive
considerado	considerate (towards others)	is considered (to be)
listo	clever	ready (to do something)
malo	bad person	tastes bad / is no longer of good quality
vivo	intense	alive

1 Sort the following examples into whether they use *ser* or *estar*.

estudiante   alto   en Egipto   enferma   francés   viviendo

ser	estar

2 Translate the sentences below, taking care to use the correct form of *ser* or *estar*.

The boy was ready. He was also a good, considerate young boy, but he was bored of his daily life and wanted to see the world.

____

____

____

____

1 From the infinitives given, write all the present subjunctive forms under the column headings.

infinitive	I	you	he / she / it / you (formal)	we	you (pl.)	they / you (pl. formal)
1 temer						
2 permitir						
3 querer						
4 mostrar						
5 empezar						
6 ver						
7 saber						

2a Underline the verbs in each sentence and write on the line below what tense they are.

1 Pero ahora me gusta ir con mi novia y a veces voy solo, es muy relajante.

____

2 Creo que mis gustos, en cuanto a las películas, continuarán cambiando durante los próximos años.

____

3 Hasta ese momento siempre iba con él.

____

4 Cuando era pequeño me gustaba ir al cine con mi padre para ver películas de dibujos animados.

____

5 También tengo muchas ganas de llevar a mi hijo al cine – pero no me apetece ser padre durante los próximos años, todavia soy demasiado joven.

____

6 Pero él se murió cuando yo tenía doce años.

____

2b Put the sentences into the correct chronological order.

1st	2nd	3rd	4th	5th	6th

2c On a separate sheet of paper, translate the sentences in their chronological order, taking care to focus on the grammar points being tested.

1 **Rellena los espacios en blanco en las frases siguientes con la forma adecuada de la palabra en paréntesis para traducir el inglés de abajo.**

1 Te recomendamos que ____________ (comprar) un traje nuevo; ____________ (ese) no te queda muy bien.

We recommend that you buy a new suit; that one doesn't suit you very well.

2 ____________ (querer) ir al cine ayer pero Juan ____________ (tener) que ir al médico.

We wanted to go to the cinema yesterday but Juan had to go to the doctor.

3 ____________ (estar) cansados y ____________ (ser) casi imposible terminar el trabajo hoy.

We're tired and it would be almost impossible to finish the work today.

4 ¿En serio? No ____________ (estar) de acuerdo. ____________ (ser) mejor cuando teníamos veinte años.

Seriously? I don't agree. It was better when we were twenty years old.

5 Estaba ____________ (explicárselo) a Laly cuando el teléfono ____________ (sonar).

I was explaining it to Laly when the phone rang.

6 ¿ ____________ (terminar) todos? ____________ (seguir) hablando pero no me gusta para nada.

Have you all finished? You keep talking but I don't like it at all.

2 **Completa esta descripción de un estudio medioambiental reciente, escogiendo palabras de la lista A–M. Escribe la letra de la palabra en la casilla.**

Un equipo internacional de científicos ha descubierto, ____________ las mediciones del satélite CryoSat de la Agencia Espacial Europea (ESA), que la superficie de hielo registrado en el Ártico de los últimos seis veranos ____________ la menor en 30 años.

Los expertos han indicado que el nivel más bajo se alcanzó el pasado mes de septiembre cuando se ____________ una superficie de 3.610.000 kilómetros cuadrados.

El hielo que cubre el Ártico ha disminuido en todas las estaciones del año

Las estimaciones, generadas por el University College de Londres, se concentran tanto en la cobertura como en el volumen del hielo marino. Y sus resultados han sugerido que el hielo ártico ha disminuido dramáticamente durante todo el año. De hecho, el volumen de hielo ha caído un 36 por ciento en otoño y un 9 por ciento en invierno, entre 2003 y 2012.

Ante ____________ cifras, el equipo de científicos ha investigado estas pérdidas durante los inviernos de 2010–11 y 2011–12. ____________ estudio ha confirmado, por primera vez, que la disminución de la cobertura de hielo marino en la región polar se ha visto ____________ por una disminución sustancial en el volumen de hielo.

No obstante, los investigadores admiten que dos años de datos de CryoSat no son ____________ de un cambio a largo plazo.

letra	palabra
A	indicativos
B	acompañar
C	este
D	utilizando
E	registró
F	estas
G	sugieren
H	acompañada
I	demostraron
J	ha estado
K	ha sido
L	resultaron
M	han indicado

Gramática

The **conditional tense** is usually translated as 'would', e.g. 'he would visit', and it implies, as its name suggests, the result of a condition, e.g. 'I would buy a yacht if I were rich.'

Points to remember:

1 The 'I' form and the 'he / she / it' form are identical – use the context to help you work out who is being referred to.

2 Events referred to with the conditional are not guaranteed to happen – they will only happen if something else happens first!

3 The conditional tense is often used with the imperfect subjunctive (see page 58) and *si* (if).

Formation

The conditional tense is easy to form: you simply add the appropriate ending to the infinitive.

I would eat	*comería*
you would eat	*comerías*
he / she / it / you (formal) would eat	*comería*
we would eat	*comeríamos*
you (pl.) would eat	*comeríais*
they / you (pl. formal) would eat	*comerían*

Consejo

Imagine a timeline. Future events move off to the right. The conditional tense refers to the future, so we need to extend the infinitive to the right by adding the ending on to the end, without taking anything off the infinitive!

Gramática

Key irregulars

(the same as for the future tense)

	infinitive	conditional stem
to say	*decir*	*dir-*
to do / make	*hacer*	*har-*
to be able to	*poder*	*podr-*
to want	*querer*	*querr-*
to go out	*salir*	*saldr-*
to have	*tener*	*tendr-*
to have*	*haber*	*habr-*

*conditional of *hay* (there is)

Point to remember:
The conditional ending is always placed after an 'r', in both regular and irregular verbs.

1 **Complete the sentences below by putting the verb in brackets into the conditional tense.**

1 Si tuviera que elegir, me ________________ ir a Barcelona este verano. (gustar)

2 No ________________ nada – es perfecto. (cambiar, nosotros)

3 ________________ un montón de opciones para todos. (haber)

4 La gente ________________ que él ha sido uno de los mejores de nuestros días. (decir)

5 Nadie ________________ negar la lógica de su argumento. (poder)

2 **On a separate sheet of paper, write an explanation for yourself of the meaning, usage and formation of the conditional tense.**

Record this on your phone as a revision tool for later on – being able to say what would happen if someone listened to you is a useful skill, both for exams and life!

Gramática

These are in fact not very radical at all!
First, a few reminders ...

The **present tense** is used to describe:

1 something that is happening now

2 something that happens on a regular basis (which may have started in the past)

Formation

For **regular** verbs:

Step 1) Remove *-ar* / *-er* / *-ir* from the infinitive.

Step 2) Add the ending for the person who is doing the action, e.g. *hablo* (I speak), *vives* (you live), *comemos* (we eat).

-ar: *hablo, hablas, habla, hablamos, habláis, hablan*

-er: *como, comes, come, comemos, coméis, comen*

-ir: *vivo, vives, vive, vivimos, vivís, viven*

The **radical-changers** – or the **1, 2, 3, 6 verbs** – are slightly different ...

Step 1) Certain letter sequences in the stem change following set patterns. **However**, they only change in four of the six forms.

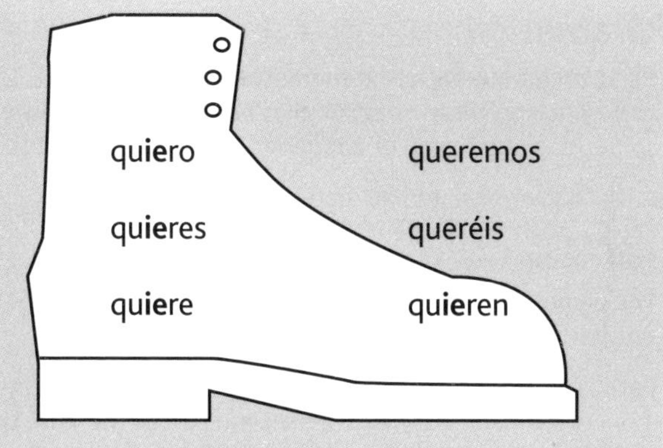

As you can see above, an easy way to remember this pattern is to think of them as the 'boot' verbs! Look at the layout.

Step 2) Add the normal, regular present tense endings.

The stem-changing patterns

o to ue Examples: *dormir (duermo), encontrar (encuentro), poder (puedo), volver (vuelvo)*

Note: *jugar* also follows this pattern, only using **u** to **ue**

e to ie Examples: *preferir (prefiero), querer (quiero), sugerir (sugiero)*

e to i Examples: *pedir (pido), decir* [also a '-go' verb] (I say = *digo*)

1 Complete the 'boot' grids for the following verbs, taking care to use the correct radical-changing pattern.

dormir (*to sleep*)
jugar (*to play*)
recomendar (*to recommend*)

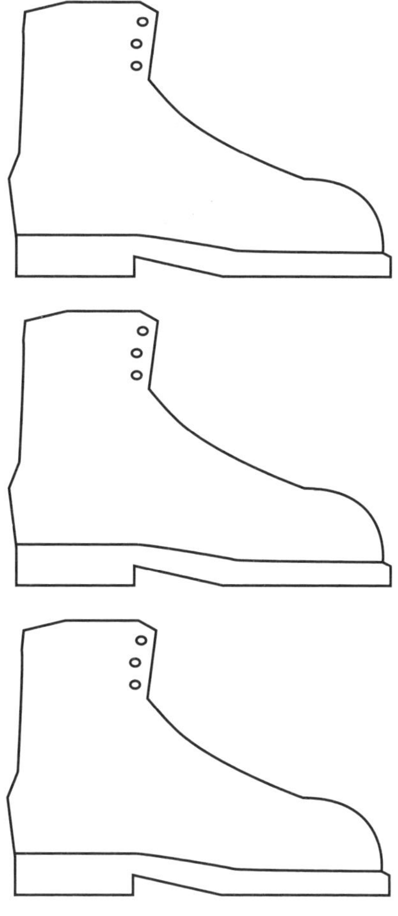

2a Find the infinitive for each of the conjugated radical-changing verbs below.

2b Write the meaning of the infinitive. Look it up if you need to.

	infinitive	meaning
1 vierten	____________	____________
2 recuerdo	____________	____________
3 confiesa	____________	____________
4 consienten	____________	____________
5 miento	____________	____________

3 On a separate sheet of paper, translate the sentences below from English into Spanish, using the verbs in brackets.

1 The boy denies (*negar*) the accusations.

2 I usually go (*soler*) to the cinema every week.

3 It begins (*empezar*) at 8.00 and the doors close (*cerrarse*) at 8.10.

4 We recommend (*recomendar*) listening to it, it's fantastic.

5 I am turning on (*encender*) the light because I want (*querer*) to see more.

Gramática

Back, back a bit, back a bit more! The **pluperfect tense** is used to describe an event or action that **had** finished, usually when something else **began** or **happened** (using the preterite).

It is usually translated as: 'had …', e.g. he had finished.

Formation

The pluperfect tense is a 'compound' tense – it has more than one part.

Part 1) *haber* in the imperfect tense (this is known as the auxiliary as it helps the second part of the verb, the past participle). See below for the forms.

Part 2) the past participle

Step 1) Remove the infinitive ending (*-ar* / *-er* / *-ir*).

Step 2) Add *-ado* for *-ar* verbs.

Add *-ido* for *-er* or *-ir* verbs.

	auxiliary	past participle
I had finished	*había*	*terminado*
you had finished	*habías*	*terminado*
he / she / it / you (formal) had finished	*había*	*terminado*
we had finished	*habíamos*	*terminado*
you (pl.) had finished	*habíais*	*terminado*
they / you (pl. formal) had finished	*habían*	*terminado*

Key irregulars

	infinitive	past participle
to say	*decir*	*dicho*
to discover	*descubrir*	*descubierto**
to write	*escribir*	*escrito*
to do / make	*hacer*	*hecho*
to go	*ir*	*ido*
to die	*morir*	*muerto*
to put	*poner*	*puesto*
to break	*romper*	*roto*
to see	*ver*	*visto*
to return	*volver*	*vuelto*

e.g. *habían visto* = they had seen

Also applies to other '-brir*' verbs, e.g. *abrir* = *abierto*

Consejo

The pluperfect tense is formed in exactly the same way as the perfect tense **except** it uses the imperfect of *haber* instead of the present. Even the irregulars are **exactly** the same.

1 Complete the table below using the pluperfect tense.

***comprar* = to buy**

English	Spanish	English	Spanish
I had bought		we had bought	
you had bought		you (pl.) had bought	
he / she / you (formal) had bought		they / you (pl. formal) had bought	

2 Draw up a similar table for the verb *fingir*, to pretend.

3a On a separate sheet of paper, write the correct past participle for each infinitive below.

1 decir
2 beber
3 completar
4 abolir
5 volver
6 ver

3b Then use each of the past participles in a pluperfect sentence using *cuando*.

Example: *Cuando había terminado los deberes llamé a Marta.*

4 On a separate sheet of paper, write an explanation for yourself of the meaning, usage and formation of the pluperfect tense.

Record this on your phone as a revision tool for later on – being able to say what had happened when something else occurred is a useful skill, both for exams and life!

Gramática

Hace … que and ***desde hace*** are used to say how long you've been doing something, or how long it is since you've done something.

1 *hace* + time phrase + *que* + *no* + present tense

This is usually used to say how long it is **since** something happened.

Hace dos meses que no me entreno.

It's two months since I've been training. (implication = has not trained since this time)

2 present tense + *desde hace* + time phrase

This is usually used to say how long something has been going on (and is still going on).

Me entreno desde hace dos meses.

I've been training for two months (implication = it's been two months and I'm still going!)

To describe an action that **was still in progress**, usually when something else happened (using *cuando*):

Step 1) Use the imperfect tense *hacía* instead of the present tense *hace*.

Step 2) Use an imperfect tense verb to describe the action that was still in progress.

Me entrenaba desde hacía dos meses.

I had been training for two months.

Points to remember:

1 If the event or action has finished use *durante* or *por*, e.g. *me entrené durante dos meses* – I trained for two months.

2 *hace* + time span = ago, e.g. *hace tres años* = three years ago

1a Decide whether each sentence below needs to use *hace* (ago), *desde* (since a precise moment), *hace … que, desde hace* or *durante* (during).

1 ______________ tres años fui a España por primera vez.

2 ______________ dos meses ______________ no veo a Juan.

3 Estudié francés ______________ casi cinco años, pero no me gustó mucho.

4 Ahorro ______________ muchos años para ir de vacaciones.

5 Quería visitar Ecuador ______________ la infancia.

6 Buscaba trabajo ______________ que había terminado los estudios.

7 Los terminé ______________ tres meses.

8 ______________ mucho tiempo que no salgo con mis amigos porque me preparo para la carrera de este viernes.

1b Translate the sentences, taking care to use good English!

1 ______________________________

2 ______________________________

3 ______________________________

4 ______________________________

5 ______________________________

6 ______________________________

7 ______________________________

8 ______________________________

Gramática

Reflexive verbs conjugate in exactly the same way as any other verb. The only difference is that they also need to use a 'reflexive pronoun'. The reflexive pronoun refers back to the subject – to whom the action is being done.

e.g. ***me*** *lavo*	= I wash [myself]	***nos*** *acostamos*	= we are going [taking ourselves] to bed
te *afeitas*	= you shave [yourself]	***os*** *ducháis*	= you (pl.) shower [yourselves]
se *levanta*	= he / she gets [him / herself] up	***se*** *lavan los dientes*	= they brush their teeth [themselves]

Word order

The reflexive pronoun goes before the verb, except in the following cases:

1 compound tenses: reflexive pronoun + *haber* + verb, e.g. *no* ***me*** *he afeitado*

2 infinitive constructions: reflexive verb + infinitive + reflexive pronoun, e.g. *voy a ducharme*

3 positive imperatives: imperative + reflexive pronoun, e.g. *¡levántate!*

4 negative imperatives: reflexive pronoun + negative imperative, e.g. *¡no* ***te*** *levantes!*

5 present participle: *estoy levantándome*

Point to remember: The addition of the extra syllable, in the form of the pronoun on the end of the verb, may require a written accent to be added to ensure stress remains in the original place.

1 **Use your knowledge of tenses to complete the grid.**

meterse – *to get involved in* **PRETERITE**			
Singular	**Meaning**	**Plural**	**Meaning**
me ____________		_____ ____________	
_____ ____________	*you got involved in*	os ____________	
_____ ____________		_____ ____________	*they / you (pl. formal) got involved in*

2a **Write the tenses of the reflexive verbs in the sentences below.**

2b **Convert the reflexive verbs into the form shown in brackets. Rewrite the whole sentence.**

1 Normalmente nos levantamos bastante tarde. tense: ____________

(yo): ________________________________

2 No se dio cuenta de la situación hasta ayer. tense: ____________

(nos): ________________________________

3 ¿Se dormían durante la película? tense: ____________

(tú): ________________________________

4 ¿Va a ponerse un abrigo? Está lloviendo. tense: ____________

(os): ________________________________

5 Se sentiría mejor después de una siesta, seguro. tense: ____________

(me): ________________________________

Gramática

Imperatives are used to give instructions or commands – to be imperious!

Formation

There are eight forms of the imperative:

positive: (Do ...!) informal (*tú / vosotros*)
formal (*usted / ustedes*)

negative: (Don't ...!) informal (*tú / vosotros*)
formal (*usted / ustedes*)

Positive commands

Informal:

tú: remove *-s* from *tú* form of present tense
e.g. *¡come!* (eat!), *¡baila!* (dance!)

Irregulars for positive *tú* form:

decir	*di*	*salir*	*sal*
hacer	*haz*	*ser*	*sé**
ir	*ve*	*tener*	*ten*
poner	*pon*	*venir*	*ven*

*Take care not to confuse this with the 'I' form of *saber* in the present tense! Normally the context will make clear which it is.

vosotros: **Step 1)** Remove *-r* from infinitive.
Step 2) Add '*d*'.
e.g. *¡comed!* (eat!), *¡bailad!* (dance!)

Formal:

usted: *usted* form of present subjunctive
e.g. *¡coma!* (eat!), *¡baile!* (dance!)

ustedes: *ustedes* form of present subjunctive
e.g. *¡coman!* (eat!), *¡bailen!* (dance!)

Negative commands

Negative word + *tú / vosotros / usted / ustedes* form of subjunctive

Negative	**Imperative**	**Form used**
No (Don't ...!)	*comas*	(*tú*)
Nunca (Never ...!)	*toméis*	(*vosotros*)
Nadie (Nobody...!)	*olvide*	(*usted*)
	pierdan	(*ustedes*)

Point to remember: Most of the time the subjunctive endings simply swap over: '*-ar*' verba use the '*-er*' present tense endings whilst '*-er*' and '*-ir*' ones use the '*-ar*' present tense endings.

Key irregulars

to say*	*decir*	*diga*
to do / make*	*hacer*	*haga*
to be able to*	*poder*	*pueda*
to want*	*querer*	*quiera*
to have*	*tener*	*tenga*

*All use the 'I' form of the present tense to form their subjunctive stem.

to have	*haber*	*haya*
to go	*ir*	*vaya*
to be	*ser*	*sea*

Point to remember: If you use an object pronoun after the imperative, e.g. *cómelo* (eat it!) you need to add an accent to maintain the existing stress pattern on the verb.

1a Conjugate the following verb + pronoun into all of the forms of the imperative in the grid below.

hablarle **– to talk to her**

	tú	**vosotros**	**usted**	**ustedes**
positive				
negative				

1b On a separate sheet of paper, do the same for the following verbs.

decírmelo – to say it to me (take care, this is irregular in the imperative!)

cerrarlo – to close it (watch out, it's a radical-changing verb!)

mirarme – to look at me

ir – to go

evitarle – to avoid him

tomarlo – to take it

Don't forget to add accents to maintain the stress on the verb.

Consejo

Remember that pronouns go on the end of positive commands, but before negative commands, e.g. *cómelo / no lo comas*. See page 31 to remind yourself.

Gramática

The **preterite tense** is the most commonly used tense. Within that, there are two sets of verbs that don't follow the regular pattern.

1 Radical-changers: where certain letter patterns change.

2 Irregulars: usually the most commonly used verbs. They become irregular because they are used so much and people want to make them 'easier' to say!

First of all, a reminder:

The preterite is used to describe a past, finished event. It is usually translated as: '-ed' in English, e.g. he waited, they phoned.

Formation

For regular verbs:

Step 1) Remove the infinitive ending (*-ar / -er / -ir*).

Step 2) Add the appropriate ending for who did the action.

	-ar	-er	-ir
I	-é	-í	-í
you	-aste	-iste	-iste
he / she / it / you (formal)	-ó	-ió	-ió
we	-amos	-imos	-imos
you (pl.)	-asteis	-isteis	-isteis
they / you (pl. formal)	-aron	-ieron	-ieron

Gramática

For radical-changers:

Step 1) Find the stem using the patterns listed below.

Step 2) Add endings as above.

Radical change only happens in the 3rd person singular and plural!

o to u *dormir (durmió), morir (murió)*

e to i *pedir (pidió), sentir (sintió), sugerir (sugirió)*

Spelling changes in the 'I' form

car to qu *buscar (bus**qu**é), sacar (sa**qu**é)*

gar to gu *llegar (lle**gu**é), pagar (pa**gu**é)*

zar to c *comenzar (comen**c**é), empezar (empe**c**é)*

guar to gü *averiguar (averi**gü**é)*

For irregular verbs:

Step 1) Use the irregular stem.

Step 2) Add the appropriate endings as listed below.

Note: where an irregular differs from the normal ending pattern it is indicated in the following list.

I	*-e*
you	*-iste*
he / she / it / you (formal)	*-o*
we	*-imos*
you (pl.)	*-isteis*
they / you (pl. formal)	*-ieron*

Irregular stems

infinitive	meaning	stem	exceptions?
andar	to walk	*anduv-*	
estar	to be	*estuv-*	
tener	to have	*tuv-*	
conducir	to drive	*conduj-*	
decir	to say	*dij-*	
traer	to bring	*traj-*	
dar	to give	*d-*	*di* = I gave
hacer	to do / make	*hic-*	*hizo* = he did
poder	to be able to	*pud-*	
poner	to put	*pus-*	
saber	to know	*sup-*	
querer	to want	*quis-*	
venir	to come	*vin-*	
ver	to see	*v-*	*vi* = I saw

The odd couple

Ser (to be) and *ir* (to go) have the **same preterite forms**:

I	*fui*
you	*fuiste*
he / she / it / you (formal)	*fue*
we	*fuimos*
you (pl.)	*fuisteis*
they / you (pl. formal)	*fueron*

Points to remember:

1 There are no accents on any irregular preterites.

2 *Haber* is also irregular – but you will use *había* (imperfect) far more often than *hubo* (preterite) as it is usually used to describe ongoing events.

1 Write the *yo* form of the preterite for each of the following infinitives.

1 estar ____________
2 advertir ____________
3 empezar ____________
4 tener ____________
5 dar ____________
6 buscar ____________
7 adivinar ____________
8 sugerir ____________
9 decir ____________
10 volver ____________

2a Categorise the following verbs into the table below.

jugar (*to play*)
aprovechar (*to make the most of*)
pagar (*to pay*)
hacer (*to do*)
consentir (*to consent*)
terminar (*to finish*)
ser (*to be*)
abrir (*to open*)
ir (*to go*)
tocar (*to touch*)
conseguir (*to achieve*)
elegir (*to choose*)

Regular	Irregular	Spelling change in 1st person preterite	Radical-changing 3rd person preterite

2b Now use five of these verbs in the preterite in sentences of your own.

1 ____________
2 ____________
3 ____________
4 ____________
5 ____________

3 Use the following five verbs to describe a relaxing past holiday.

ir decidir darse cuenta ver comenzar

____
____
____
____

4 On a separate sheet of paper, write an explanation for yourself of the different patterns used to form the preterite tense.

Record this on your phone as a revision tool for later on – being able to say what happened using a variety of preterite forms is a useful skill, both for exams and life!

Gramática

The **future tense** is usually translated as 'will', e.g. he **will** visit.

Points to remember:

1 All of the irregulars are exactly the same as for the conditional tense.

2 This tense is usually used for an action that is not imminent, or in the near future. The immediate future (*voy a* + infinitive) is used in these instances.

Formation

Simply add the appropriate ending to the infinitive.

I will eat	*comer**é***
you will eat	*comer**ás***
he / she / it / you (formal) will eat	*comer**á***
we will eat	*comer**emos***
you (pl.) will eat	*comer**éis***
they / you (pl. formal) will eat	*comer**án***

Key irregulars
(the same as for the conditional tense)

	infinitive	**future stem**
to say	*decir*	*dir-*
to do / make	*hacer*	*har-*
to be able to	*poder*	*podr-*
to want	*querer*	*querr-*
to go out	*salir*	*saldr-*
to have	*tener*	*tendr-*
to have*	*haber*	*habr-*

*future of *hay* (there is)

Point to remember: The future ending is always placed after an 'r', in both the regular and irregular forms.

Consejo

Imagine a timeline. Think of yourself doing a certain action, like eating, in different tenses, and try to picture the different verb endings, especially the future tense, added to the infinitive. Say them to yourself!

1a Separate the word snake into ten future tense verbs.

1b Write the meaning of each verb.

1c Write the infinitive for each verb.

1d On the lines on the next page use each future tense example in a sentence.

comerásdiránviviréquerremosalquilarédependerásorprenderéisaclararéhabrárecibiremos

	Future tense	Meaning	Infinitive
1			
2			
3			
4			
5			
6			
7			
8			
9			
10			

1 ______________________________

2 ______________________________

3 ______________________________

4 ______________________________

5 ______________________________

6 ______________________________

7 ______________________________

8 ______________________________

9 ______________________________

10 ______________________________

2 **Put the verbs in brackets into the future tense to complete the sentences below.**

1 En junio todos ______________ (tener) que hacer el examen – ______________ (ser) importante sacar buenas notas.

In June you will all have to do the exam – it will be important to get good marks.

2 Te ______________ (ver) mañana e ______________ (ir) a la biblioteca – necesito tu ayuda.

I'll see you tomorrow and we'll go to the library – I need your help.

3 ¿Cuándo ______________ (llegar)? Les ______________ (llamar) a las cinco para saber los detalles.

When will you arrive? We will call you at 5 to find out the details.

4 En el futuro ______________ (lograr) mucho pero antes ______________ (hacer) falta esforzarte un poco más.

In the future you will achieve a lot, but first you will need to make a bit more effort.

5 ______________ (poder) utilizar fuentes de energía menos nocivas, algo que ______________ (proteger) el futuro del planeta para nuestros hijos.

We will be able to use less harmful sources of energy, something that will protect the future of the planet for our children.

3 **On a separate sheet of paper, write an explanation for yourself about how to form the future tense and precisely what it means. Make sure you explain the irregulars and when you would use the future tense compared to the immediate future!**

Record this on your phone as a revision tool for later on – being able to say what will happen in a situation, or what you will do, is a useful skill, both for exams and life!

1a Find the 20 verb forms hidden in the wordsearch grid.

1b Write them into the table under the correct tense headings.

1c Write the infinitive for each verb.

1d Translate each verb.

h	o	a	p	s	w	a	u	y	a	t	e	h	a	p
a	a	d	b	i	d	i	e	r	n	a	p	i	c	r
m	l	b	i	a	e	á	r	d	l	a	v	o	t	e
l	m	e	í	s	n	n	g	n	a	í	m	o	c	f
e	i	o	r	a	i	i	s	n	d	t	q	d	p	i
j	u	e	g	o	v	a	v	a	e	b	u	r	e	e
e	a	a	o	e	r	i	í	i	n	h	e	u	t	r
t	t	a	b	a	o	m	s	b	d	p	r	e	n	e
e	s	r	t	l	a	e	e	t	a	a	r	a	í	l
s	u	b	i	e	r	o	n	r	o	h	í	l	b	r
d	i	r	e	m	o	s	a	h	e	r	a	t	i	b
f	u	i	s	t	e	r	i	b	d	z	s	v	r	r
h	u	e	l	e	í	t	n	n	t	a	c	i	c	t
r	t	f	s	a	í	r	e	u	q	d	e	o	s	r
c	u	b	r	i	ó	t	n	o	w	r	a	t	e	m

1e On a separate sheet of paper, write six sentences, each one using a verb from a different column of the table.

Pluperfect x2	Imperfect x3	Preterite x5	Present x5	Future x2	Conditional x3
verb:	verb:	verb:	verb:	verb:	verb:
inf:	inf:	inf:	inf:	inf:	inf:
trans:	trans:	trans:	trans:	trans:	trans:
verb	verb	verb	verb	verb	verb
inf:	inf:	inf:	inf:	inf:	inf:
trans:	trans:	trans:	trans:	trans:	trans:
	verb	verb	verb		verb
	inf:	inf:	inf:		inf:
	trans:	trans:	trans:		trans:
		verb	verb		
		inf:	inf:		
		trans:	trans:		
		verb	verb		
		inf:	inf:		
		trans:	trans:		

2a Be creative and describe the scene in the image, imagining that you took the photo.

Ensure that you use at least …

- 3 preterite tense verbs
- 3 imperfect tense verbs
- 3 conditional tense verbs
- 2 subjunctive phrases
- an idiomatic *ser* or *estar* phrase
- 2 demonstrative adjectives or pronouns
- 2 negatives

2b Now mark your description using the grid below. Every time you use that grammar point award yourself that number of points!

Grammar point	Points per use	Times used	Total score for that point
negative	1		
adjective (with correct word order + agreement)	1		
preterite tense verb	2		
imperfect tense verb	2		
demonstrative adjective / pronoun	2		
immediate future verb (*voy a* + infinitive)	3		
conditional tense verb	3		
idiomatic *ser / estar* phrase	3		
por / para	4		
subjunctive phrase	5		
			Total:

2c Now write two more sentences below to add at least 20 more points.

1 **Completa esta descripción de los problemas con la sal, escogiendo las palabras de la lista A–M. Escribe la letra de la palabra en los espacios en blanco. ¡Ojo! No necesitarás todas las palabras.**

Nadie duda a ______________ alturas de que el tabaco es perjudicial para la salud, que por nuestro bien hay que dejar de fumar.

Pero de la sal no pensamos lo mismo. Por herencia histórica, no tenemos mala opinión de la sal. Y sin embargo, al reducir a la mitad el consumo de sal diario de nuestra dieta se ______________ beneficios para nuestra salud comparables a los derivados de dejar de fumar.

La comparación ______________ hacen los expertos médicos de la Fundación Española del Corazón (FEC), que nos recuerdan que el consumo excesivo de sal es responsable de numerosos problemas de salud, no sólo de los relacionados con las enfermedades cardiovasculares, sino también con el cáncer de estómago.

______________ más de una década que la Organización Mundial de la Salud (OMS) ______________ en 6g el consumo máximo diario de sal, cifra muy ______________ debajo de la que se ingiere de media en el mundo (también en España), entre 10g y 12g. La mayor parte de la ingesta diaria de sal, el 80%, ______________ de los productos envasados y precocinados.

La Sociedad Española de Cardiología considera que reducir el consumo de sal es responsabilidad de todos: del ciudadano (que debe empezar a cocinar sin sal), de la industria alimentaria (que debería disminuir la cantidad de sal que se añade a los productos) y de las administraciones públicas (que deberían tomar medidas restrictivas ______________ con el consumo de sal).

A	relacionadas		H	por
B	hace		I	el
C	obtendrá		J	obtendrán
D	proviene		K	para
E	la		L	estos
F	estableció		M	desde hace
G	estas			

2 **Completa esta descripción de un estudio medioambiental reciente, escogiendo palabras de la lista A–M. Escribe la letra de la palabra en la casilla.**

Una de las tres parlamentarias más jóvenes de México se ha encontrado en el centro de una polémica sexista. Al llevar una minifalda la diputada federal del PRD, de 23 años, provocó acusaciones de que su imagen le importa más ______________ ser productiva en materia legislativa. En México, donde existen leyes para asegurar la representación proporcional, una veintena de legisladoras ______________ eliminar contenidos sexistas.

Las diputadas pidieron que se ______________ con la reproducción de este tipo de contenidos en los que se habla de la apariencia de las legisladoras.

La reacción de las diputadas ______________ a las declaraciones de Tovar, ______________ declaró en una entrevista para Milenio TV que hay que ir erradicando la cultura machista al tiempo que reivindicó su labor en la Cámara.

'Me gustaría que se enfocaran en mi trabajo legislativo en lugar de la imagen', ______________ horas después de que sus compañeras ______________ filas por el caso. Criticó la continuación de un machismo exacerbado en México y además rechazó la actitud misógina y discriminatoria que predomina.

A	al		H	sucedió
B	cerraran		I	que
C	dijo		J	acabe
D	dice		K	cerraron
E	pidieron		L	quien
F	con		M	acaba
G	de			

Topic 4: Possessive adjectives and pronouns

Singular		Plural	
Masculine	**Feminine**	**Masculine**	**Feminine**
mi	mi	mis	mis
tu	tu	tus	tus
su	su	sus	sus
nuestro	nuestra	nuestros	nuestras
vuestro	vuestra	vuestros	vuestras
su	su	sus	sus

Gramática

Possessive adjectives

- indicate possession – who something belongs to
- must agree with the noun
- have the same form for masculine and feminine **except** in the *nuestro* and *vuestro* forms.

Gramática

Possessive pronouns

- indicate possession
- agree with the noun
- need to use the definite article (*el / la / los / las*)
- do not use the definite article when following *ser*

e.g. *Pedro admitió que el problema es suyo.* (Pedro admitted that the problem is his.)

- If there is any ambiguity in the sentence (i.e it is not clear to whom *la suya* etc. refers), use *la de él / ella / ustedes*, etc.

1a **Rewrite the nouns below, inserting the correct possessive adjective as indicated in brackets. Think carefully about the gender of the noun.**

1b Translate 1–5 into English.

1 mentalidad (**vosotros**) __________ __________

2 problemas (**yo**) __________ __________

3 perfil (**tú**) __________ __________

4 opiniones (**nosotros**) __________ __________

5 crisis (**vosotros**) __________ __________

	Masc. sing.	Fem. sing.	Masc. pl.	Fem. pl.
mine	el mío	la mía	los míos	las mías
yours	el tuyo	la tuya	los tuyos	las tuyas
his / hers / its / yours (formal)	el suyo	la suya	los suyos	las suyas
ours	el nuestro	la nuestra	los nuestros	las nuestras
yours (pl.)	el vuestro	la vuestra	los vuestros	las vuestras
theirs / yours (pl. formal)	el suyo	la suya	los suyos	las suyas

2a Reorder the words below to make sentences.

1 familia al de lado suya Madrid en vivía mi la __________

2 coche mi cerca del había dejado tuyo __________

3 equipo juega su nuestra la que en misma la liga __________

4 niega nadie suyas son que __________

5 problema míos el es que perdido he los __________

6 daros cuenta diferencia deberíais la entre vuestros suyos y de los los __________

7 sean creo que no tuyas opiniones mis firmes tan como las __________

8 utilizado junio desde que ha empezó la en mía __________

2b On a separate sheet of paper, translate the sentences.

Gramática

Relative pronouns

These are used to connect two parts of a sentence when the two parts refer to the same noun.

They are **never** omitted, unlike in English.

e.g. *Vi el partido del que hablabas* (I saw the match [that] you were talking about).

que

- the most commonly used relative pronoun
- means 'who', 'that', 'whom' or 'which'
- refers to people or things
- can introduce a subject (whoever / whatever is doing the action), e.g. *el chico que es guapo* (the boy that / who is good looking): it's the boy who is doing the looking good!
- can introduce an object (whoever / whatever is having the action done to them / it), e.g. *el chico que quiero* (the boy that I love): the boy is being loved but has no active role.

quien

- only refers to people
- means 'who'/'whom'
- used after a preposition (*a, de, en, con*) instead of *que*, e.g. *el chico con quien voy a la piscina es muy guapo* (the boy with whom I go to the pool is very good looking)
- plural form = *quienes*, and there is no change for feminine forms, e.g. *las amigas con quienes normalmente voy de compras*
- *quien* can be replaced by *que* or *a quien* (depending on your personal choice) when:
  1. it is describing a person
  2. it is being used as the direct object pronoun, e.g. *el chico que vi ayer / el chico a quien vi ayer* (the boy that / who I saw yesterday)

el que / la que / los que / las que

- used after prepositions *a, de, en, con*
- often used to avoid ambiguity when more than one noun is included in the sentence, e.g. *el chico con el que fuiste al baile* (the boy that you went to the dance with)

el cual / la cual / los cuales / las cuales

- mean 'which'
- used after all other prepositions apart from *a, de, en* or *con*, e.g. *al lado de* (next to), *antes de* (before), *detrás de* (behind), *dentro de* (inside), *después de* (after), e.g. *el chico al lado del cual estaba sentado* (the boy next to whom I was sitting)

lo que

- used to refer to a general idea rather than a specific object, e.g. *lo que más me molesta* (that which annoys me most)

Relative adjectives

- *cuyo / cuya / cuyos / cuyas*
- 'whose' – the sentence usually contains an owner and a noun that is owned
- agrees with the noun that is owned, **not** the owner, e.g. *el chico, cuyos padres son franceses, es muy guapo* (the boy, whose parents are French, is very good looking)

1 **Categorise the conditions below into the relative pronouns and adjectives table to indicate the usage of each form.**

Used after prepositions *a*, *de*, *en* and *con*	Can be used either as a subject or object pronoun
Used after all prepositions except *a*, *de*, *en* and *con*	'Whose'
Used when *que* might be ambiguous	Only refers to people
Refers to people or things	Used to describe an abstract, general concept
Sentence contains an owner and something owned	Agrees with the owned noun

Relative pronoun or adjective	Usage
que	
quien	
el que etc.	

el cual etc.	
lo que	
cuyo etc.	

2 **Draw lines to match up the beginnings (1–6) and the endings (a–f) of these sentences.**

1 Simón es el chico
2 Son los amigos
3 Simón es mi amigo
4 Son los que
5 Lo que
6 La boda tendrá lugar en una iglesia,

a me sorprende es que van a casarse el viernes.
b con quienes juego a cartas a veces.
c al lado de la cual se podrán sacar unas fotos muy bonitas.
d que es productor de documentales.
e que va a casarse con Sofía.
f viven en Londres.

3 **Translate the following sentences.**

1 It's the house inside which nobody has stepped [*entrar*] since 1978.

____

2 Look who's arriving!

____

3 There are a lot of things that you can do.

____

4 Unfortunately, what I want to do is impossible.

____

5 My friend who used to live in the house next to yours lives in Spain now.

____

6 My two friends, those who have just got married, have decided to visit my uncle, whose house is enormous.

____

____

Gramática

In Topic 2 we looked at the **subjunctive**, the 'mood' that we use in specific conditions. You need to know **when** to use it. Look back at page 34 to remind yourself.

Expressions of purpose always require a subjunctive. *Para que* is one of the most commonly used subjunctive introducers:

Te doy este dinero para que vayas de viaje.

I'm giving you this money so that you can go travelling.

There are also some set phrases where the subjunctive must be used:

digan lo que digan = whatever they might say

sea lo que sea = whatever it might be

pase lo que pase = whatever might happen

1a **Complete the sentences below with either the present subjunctive or the present indicative, using the verb provided in brackets.**

1 Quiero que me ______________ (enviar – ellos) algo de Barcelona.

2 Estoy trabajando mucho para que ______________ (ir – nosotros) de vacaciones este verano.

3 Cuando ______________ (llegar – tú) te cuento de la película – te recomiendo que la ______________ (ver – tú) muy pronto.

4 Tal vez ______________ (comprar – yo) un coche nuevo, pero ______________ (depender – él) de muchos factores y ______________ (deber – nosotros) considerarlo con cuidado.

5 ______________ (decir – ellos) lo que ______________ (decir – ellos), creo que ______________ (tener – yo) que hacerlo.

1b **On a separate sheet of paper, explain why you have chosen each mood.**

Gramática

Formation

Check back on page 33 for the formation of the present subjunctive for regular and irregular verbs.

Other examples:

-car: *buscar* (to look for), *tocar* (to touch)

-gar: *rogar* (to beg), *jugar* (to play) [but still uses its radical change, i.e. *juegue*]

-zar: *empezar* (to begin), *rezar* (to pray), *forzar* (to force)

-guar: *apaciguar* (to pacify)

Spelling change verbs

car to *qu* e.g. *sacar – sa**que***

gar to *gu* e.g. *llegar – lle**gue***

zar to *c* e.g. *comenzar – comience*

guar to *gü* e.g. *averiguar – averi**güe***

A few more irregulars – the accented ones

There is one special verb that has an accent on the 1st and 3rd person forms of the singular:

dar (to give): *dé, des, dé, demos, deis, den*

Note that *estar* also has accents on all forms **except** 'we':

estar (to be): *esté, estés, esté, estemos, estéis, estén*

2a **Conjugate the infinitives below into the requested form of the present subjunctive, thinking carefully about whether they are regular, irregular, radical-changing or spelling change verbs.**

1 aconsejar (*yo*) ______________

2 dar (*ellas*) ______________

3 empezar (*nosotros*) ______________

4 prometer (*tú*) ______________

5 querer (*él*) ______________

6 ir (*vosotros*) ______________

7 forzar (*usted*) ______________

8 ignorar (*tú*) ______________

2b **On a separate sheet of paper, use five of the subjunctives in sentences, ensuring that you pick a different reason to use a subjunctive for each sentence.**

Gramática

The **passive** is used a lot in English. It describes what has happened **to** something or somebody.

e.g. he was robbed – 'he' did nothing

it was smashed by vandals – 'it' did nothing

In Spanish the passive 'voice' is often avoided.

Ways of avoiding the passive

1 **Use *se*.**

On page 21 we studied how to form and use *se* to replace the passive.

Formation

se + 3rd person **singular or plural**

e.g.

passive: *Fue robado*

active: *Se le robó* = someone robbed him.

passive: *Esos caramelos son vendidos en la tienda.*

active: *Esos caramelos se venden en la tienda* = Those sweets are sold in the shop.

2 **Make the sentence active.**

passive: *La tienda fue destruida por unos vándalos.* (The shop did nothing!)

active: *Unos vándalos destruyeron la tienda.* (The vandals actively destroyed the shop.)

1 Rewrite the following sentences, using either *se* or an active verb to replace the passive.

1 La conferencia ha sido organizada por unos expertos.

____

2 La ciudad fue destruida por los romanos hace casi dos mil años.

____

3 Fue perdido como resultado de unos errores graves.

____

4 Será entregado el lunes por uno de nuestros agentes locales.

____

5 Ha sido visitado por tanta gente que ahora está demasiado cansado.

____

6 Alguien fue detenido esta mañana, aunque su identidad es protegida por la policía.

____

7 El equipo está patrocinado por una compañía local.

____

8 Fuimos parados por los aduaneros y nuestras maletas fueron examinadas.

____

Gramática

We have now studied four tenses used to describe the past: the perfect, imperfect, preterite and pluperfect.

It is important to always use each tense in the correct situation.

	Perfect	**Imperfect**	**Preterite**	**Pluperfect**
Meaning	have ...ed	was / used to	...ed	had ...ed
Used to describe	recently finished events / actions	ongoing or habitual actions in the past. Often interrupted by a preterite action.	past, finished events	an event that had finished **when** something else happened. A step back in time.
Definitely ended?	yes	no	yes	yes
Compound tense (more than 1 word)?	yes	no	no	yes
Formation: Step 1)	*haber* in present tense (*he, has, ha, hemos, habéis, han*)	Remove *-ar / -er / -ir*.	Remove *-ar / -er / -ir*.	*haber* in imperfect tense (*había, habías, había, habíamos, habíais, habían*)
Formation: Step 2)	past participle: **minus** *-ar*, **add** *-ado* **minus** *-er / -ir* **add** *-ido*	*-ar:* add *-aba, -abas, -aba, -ábamos, -abais, -aban* *-er / -ir:* add *-ía, -ías, -ía, -íamos, íais, -ían*	*-ar:* add *-é, -aste, -ó, -amos, -asteis, -aron* *-er / -ir:* add *-í, -iste, -ió, -imos, -isteis, -ieron*	past participle: **minus** *-ar*, **add** *-ado* **minus** *-er / -ir* **add** *-ido*

1a Find the past tense verbs in the word snake and, on a separate sheet of paper, categorise them by tense (perfect, imperfect, preterite, pluperfect).

1b On a separate sheet of paper, translate the words you found in the word snake.

vivierondestruyóhabíanasistidoañadíamoshaaprovechadohemospersuadidobailabassupisteexistíahabíashecho

2a Underline the conjugated verbs used in each sentence.

1. Cuando fui a la playa con mis primos nos encontramos a un amigo que no habíamos visto desde hace mucho tiempo.
2. Me entrenaba para un triatlón cuando me torcí la rodilla y tuve que descansar durante casi un mes.
3. Lo he organizado todo: esta mañana llamé a tu madre y ya me ha dado tu pasaporte.
4. En el pasado han probado muchas cosas para intentar divertirse.

2b Identify the tenses.

2c Explain why each verb has been used in the tense that it has.

Topic 4: The imperfect subjunctive

Gramática

The **imperfect subjunctive** is only used when the conditions for a subjunctive, as explained on page 34, are met!

If they are met, an imperfect subjunctive is used.

1 When the verb in the main clause is in the imperfect, pluperfect, preterite or conditional tense.

2 When the action has **not** been completed or might happen in the future.

e.g. *No creía que fueras capaz de lograr tus objetivos.*

or when using *si* (if):

si + imperfect subjunctive + conditional

Si tuviera la oportunidad, me encantaría vivir en Barcelona.

= If I had the opportunity, I would love to live in Barcelona.

Formation

The imperfect subjunctive has two possible sets of endings: *-se* and *-ra*. It's fine to learn one of the sets of endings only, for your own use, but you should be able to recognise the other set.

Step 1) Find the 'they' form of the preterite (3rd person plural).

Step 2) Remove the *-ron*.

Step 3) Add the imperfect subjunctive endings.

-ar		-er / -ir	
hablar = to speak		vivir = to live	
hablara	hablase	viviera	viviese
hablaras	hablases	vivieras	vivieses
hablara	hablase	viviera	viviese
habláramos	hablásemos	viviéramos	viviésemos
hablarais	hablaseis	vivierais	vivieseis
hablaran	hablasen	vivieran	viviesen

Gramática

Points to remember:

1 There is no difference in meaning between the *-ra* and the *-se* forms.

2 There are no irregular imperfect subjunctives. Those verbs which are irregular in the preterite (e.g. *ir* – to go) still follow the regular pattern for imperfect subjunctives:

Step 1) Find the 'they' form of the preterite: *fueron.*

Step 2) Remove the *-ron* ending: *fue.*

Step 3) Add the imperfect subjunctive ending.

e.g. 'I' form ending = *-ra*

'I' form of imperfect subjunctive = ***fuera***

1 Complete the grid below to practise forming the imperfect subjunctive.

Infinitive	1 3rd person plural of preterite	2 Remove *-ron*	3 Form imperfect subjunctive requested
bailar	bailaron	baila	(yo) bailara
vivir			(tú)
ganar			(vosotras)
poder			(ellos)
querer			(él)
ser			(nosotros)
tocar			(usted)
dormir			(ustedes)
seguir			(ella)
comprender			(yo)
existir			(él)

2 The most common use of the imperfect subjunctive is in '*si* clauses'. Insert the imperfect subjunctive and a conditional in the spaces below. Remember, *si* + imperfect subjunctive + conditional!

1 Si ____________ (poder) elegir, ____________ (preferir) ir al Caribe.

2 Creo que mi hermano ____________ (buscar) otro trabajo si ____________ (tener) más confianza.

3 ____________ (ir) de compras si ____________ (ganar) un poco más de dinero.

4 Si mis amigos ____________ (saber) la verdad, ____________ (ser) un alivio enorme.

5 ____________ (vivir) aquí con nosotros si ____________ (conseguir) los papeles.

6 Yo ____________ (casarse) con ella si ____________ (poder).

7 Si ____________ (estudiar) aun un poco más, me parece que sus notas ____________ (mejorar) rápidamente.

8 Aunque me llevo bastante bien con mis padres, nos ____________ (llevar) mejor si ____________ (haber) un poco más de espacio en casa.

9 ____________ (enfadarse) mucho si ____________ (perder) el móvil; siempre lo lleva consigo y lo usa casi sin parar.

10 Si ____________ (dejar) de envenenarte con el tabaco ____________ (sentirse) más sano y ____________ (tener) mucho más dinero porque no ____________(gastar) tanto cada semana en comprar cigarrillos.

Topic 4: Subjunctives in different tenses

Gramática

Although the present subjunctive is the most commonly used form of the subjunctive, there are other forms as well. However, these subjunctives are still subject to the rules of use explained on page 34.

In order to know when to use the different forms of the subjunctive, the following table might help.

Main clause	Subordinate clause (containing the subjunctive)
Present tense Perfect tense Future tense	Present subjunctive • if the action is ongoing or in the future Perfect subjunctive (present subjunctive of *haber* + past participle) • if the action has been completed, e.g. *Me alegro que el trabajo haya terminado.*
Imperfect tense Pluperfect tense Preterite tense Conditional tense (*si* clause)	Imperfect subjunctive • if the action has **not** been completed or might happen in the future, e.g. *No creía que viviera contigo.* • often used in *si* clauses: *si* + imperfect subjunctive + conditional, e.g. *Si fuera primer ministro, haría mucho más para el medio ambiente.* Pluperfect subjunctive (imperfect subjunctive of *haber* + past participle) • if the action had been completed, e.g. *Si no hubiera llegado tan tarde, no habríamos perdido el tren.*

1 **Complete the crossword below using the clues given.**

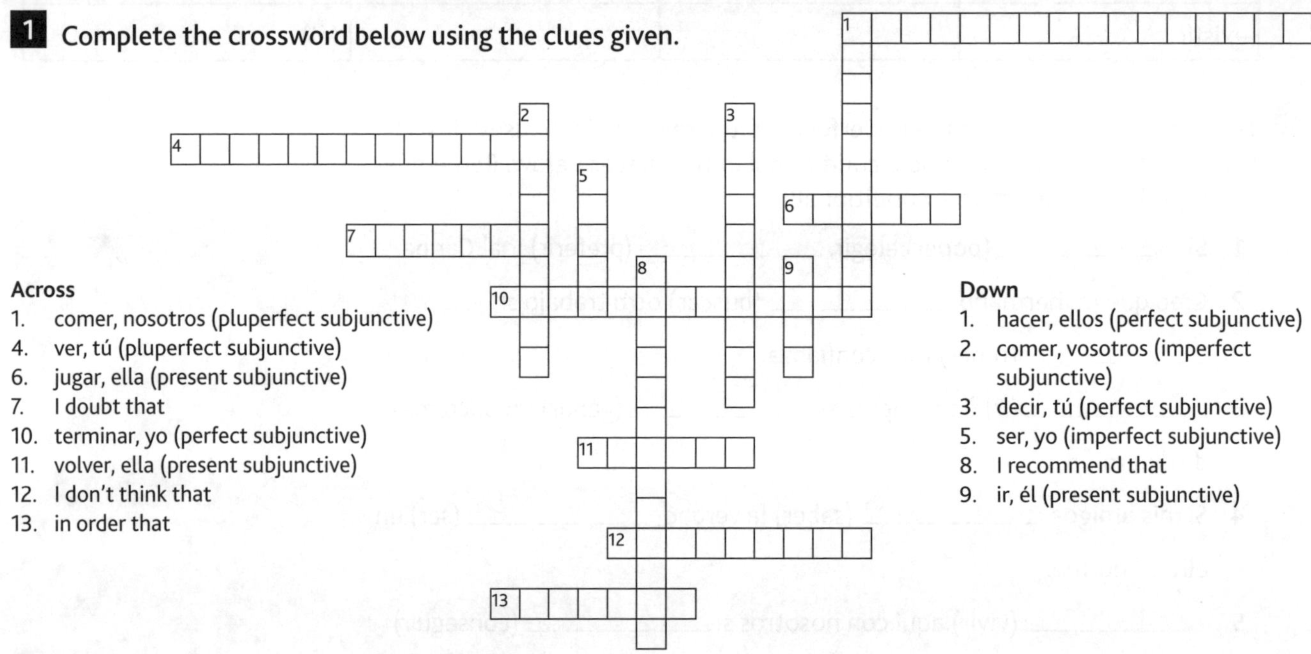

Across

1. comer, nosotros (pluperfect subjunctive)
4. ver, tú (pluperfect subjunctive)
6. jugar, ella (present subjunctive)
7. I doubt that
10. terminar, yo (perfect subjunctive)
11. volver, ella (present subjunctive)
12. I don't think that
13. in order that

Down

1. hacer, ellos (perfect subjunctive)
2. comer, vosotros (imperfect subjunctive)
3. decir, tú (perfect subjunctive)
5. ser, yo (imperfect subjunctive)
8. I recommend that
9. ir, él (present subjunctive)

2 **Complete the sentences below using an appropriate form of the subjunctive. There may be more than one correct version, but think carefully about the rules of use for each tense.**

1 Sólo querrá salir contigo cuando ____________ (cambiar) tu actitud.

2 Sugirió que ____________ (llamar) a tu padre porque lleváis mucho tiempo sin hablar.

3 Era importante que ____________ (preparar) todos los trámites antes de tu llegada.

4 El problema con toda esta situación es que dudo que ____________ (venir), ____________ (hacer) lo que ____________ (hacer).

5 Espero que un día te ____________ (dar) cuenta de cuánto me has herido.

6 Me sorprende que ____________ (decidir) aceptar su propuesta.

7 Si ____________ (decir) algo diferente te ayudaría, pero así no puedo hacer nada.

8 Juanma trabajaba mucho para que su hijo ____________ (estudiar) en un instituto privado – y eso significó que casi nunca le veía.

Gramática

algo: 'something'

- does not agree with any noun
- can be used ...
  - alone, e.g. *olvidé algo*
  - + an adjective, e.g. *es algo preocupante*
  - + *de* + infinitive, e.g. *¿Quieres algo de comer?*

alguien: 'somebody'

- does not agree with the noun
- can be used ...
  - alone, e.g. *alguien debe decir algo*
  - + *que* + subjunctive, e.g. *quiero a alguien que me aprecie*

alguno (algún) / alguna / algunos / algunas: 'somebody'

- agrees with the noun, e.g. *algunas personas*
- *Alguno* becomes *algún* before a masculine, singular noun, e.g. *algún escritor.*

ninguno (ningún) / ninguna: 'not one' / 'no'

- can only be used in the plural form (*ningunos / ningunas*) when the noun it is with **only** exists in the plural, e.g. *gafas*
- agrees with the noun
- *Ninguno* becomes *ningún* before a masculine, singular noun, e.g. *no hay ningún castillo en la región.*

mucho (many / lots), ***poco*** (a bit / few), ***todo*** (all), ***tanto*** (as many, so much), ***otro*** (other), ***cualquier*** (any), ***varios*** (various)

- All agree with the noun they describe (in adjective form) or replace (in pronoun form).
- *Tanto* shortens to *tan* before an adjective.

1 **Draw lines to join the two halves of the sentences below.**

1 Hay algo
2 Hay alguien
3 Hay algunas
4 Hay algunos
5 No hay ninguna

a personas esperándote fuera.
b razón para justificar ni su presencia ni por su actitud.
c especial en la cocina.
d esperándote fuera y parece estar de muy mal humor.
e chicos fuera y no están contentos.

2 **Complete the sentences below with the appropriate indefinite adjective or pronoun to match the English translations.**

1 Desde mi punto de vista debe ser ______________ inteligente.
From my point of view, it must be someone intelligent.

2 ______________ ha pasado para cambiar mi perspectiva.
Something has happened to change my perspective.

3 ______________ hombre tiene el derecho de ser infiel.
No man has the right to be unfaithful.

4 No puede ser ______________ importante como para que tengas que abandonar a tu familia.
It can't be so important that you have to leave your family.

5 Hay ______________ sectores de esta sociedad que quieren rechazar estos cambios recientes.
There are some parts of this society that want to reject these recent changes.

6 ______________ gente cree que cada individuo tiene el derecho de casarse, sea cual sea su sexualidad.
Many people believe that each individual has the right to get married, whatever his / her sexuality.

7 En mi opinión el plan merece ______________ vistazo.
In my opinion, the plan deserves another look.

Topic 4: Recognising the future perfect and conditional perfect tenses

Gramática

The **future perfect** is used for saying that something **will have** happened.

It is formed with the future tense of *haber* + past participle.

Point to remember: *haber* has an irregular stem in the future and conditional tenses: ***habr-***

e.g. *habrán terminado* = they **will have** finished

The **conditional perfect** is used to say that something **would have** happened.

It is formed with the conditional tense of *haber* + past participle.

e.g. *habrían terminado* = they **would have** finished

1a **Underline the future perfect or conditional perfect verb in each sentence.**

1b **In the column provided, write which tense has been used.**

1c **Translate the sentence in the box below.**

		Future perfect (FP) or conditional perfect (CP)?
1	Habremos terminado antes de las ocho, os lo juro.	
Translation		
2	Habrían continuado pero la lluvia era demasiado fuerte.	
Translation		
3	Habríamos ganado si el árbitro hubiera entendido las reglas.	
Translation		
4	Te habrían respetado más si no hubieras sido tan maleducada.	
Translation		
5	Yo te habría dejado hace unos años pero necesitabas mi ayuda.	
Translation		
6	Habréis conocido a mucha gente durante vuestros viajes.	
Translation		

2 **On a separate sheet of paper, classify the following verbs into four categories: future, conditional, future perfect and conditional perfect.**

habríamos sido	vivirán	sería	me gustaría	habrá llegado
habré comido	tendrán	pondríais	habremos visto	habría terminado

Future	Conditional	Future perfect	Conditional perfect

1 Translate the sentences below into English.

1 Si mis padres se divorciaran tendria que decidir con quién vivir.

2 Saldremos cuando hayas terminado los deberes.

3 El ciclista no habia probado ninguna sustancia ilegal.

4 No hemos comido en ese restaurante desde hace muchos meses.

5 Ni en mis sueños me habría imaginado vivir en un lugar tan bonito.

6 Iba al colegio cuando vi el accidente. Oí unos gritos escalofriantes.

7 Es esencial que admitas la verdad para que cambiemos la politica.

2 Translate the sentences below into Spanish.

1 I think that divorce is too easy nowadays.

2 If somebody attacked my brother I would want revenge.

3 That one over there is the girl whose brothers are in prison.

4 Whatever people might say, I want you to follow your desires – this life is very short.

5 In the past nobody used to talk about sustainable tourism, but it's essential for the survival of many parts of the planet.

6 If only it was possible in real life – unfortunately, nobody has asked me the same thing.

Grammar point	Points per use
Present tense	1
Hace / desde hace	1
Preterite tense	2
Indefinite adjectives / pronouns	2
Ser / estar	2
Por / para	2
Relative adjectives / pronouns	3
Present subjunctive	4
Imperfect subjunctive	5
Perfect / pluperfect subjunctive	6

3 On a separate sheet of paper, write a short paragraph of up to 50 words on each of the topics mentioned below, ensuring that your sentences include enough complexity to achieve at least 20 points per answer.

Use the points chart to test your level of writing.

- el matrimonio gay
- el turismo sostenible
- las drogas en el deporte
- el tabaco
- la destrucción de la familia tradicional
- el mundo sin colegio
- los padres juveniles
- la adopción

1 **Completa esta descripción de la importancia de comer en familia, escogiendo palabras de la lista A–M. Escribe la letra de la palabra en la casilla.**

La alimentación es una parte fundamental de lo que llamamos un estilo de vida saludable. Y pese a vivir en una sociedad desarrollada, comer bien comienza a no resultar tan fácil.

La familia siempre fue el núcleo que procuraba una buena alimentación, basada en la dieta mediterránea. Y ese buen hábito se ______________ perdiendo.

Por ello es tan importante comer en familia. Hasta el punto de que hacerlo al menos tres veces por semana reduce en los niños un 32% el riesgo de que ______________ un trastorno alimentario y un 15% el peligro de padecer obesidad.

'No hay que negociar con la comida. Es cierto que no es aconsejable obligar al niño a comer algo que no quiere, sin embargo, tampoco podemos caer en la trampa de la negociación, ______________ que coma solo aquello que le es grato,' recalca. Admite también que si a negociar cada elemento de nuestras vidas nunca ______________ nada.

La experta de la Sociedad Española de Endocrinología y Nutrición explica la importancia que tiene que los niños ______________ ocho horas y ______________ ejercicio físico.

letra	palabra
A	está
B	duermen
C	duerman
D	sufran
E	conseguiríamos
F	es
G	fuéramos
H	admitiendo
I	realicen
J	hacen
K	estaba
L	sufrir

2 **Rellena los espacios en el texto siguiente con la forma adecuada de la palabra en paréntesis.**

Más de 50.000 toneladas de comida fresca de los supermercados acaban cada año en la basura porque Sanidad prohíbe que **a** ____________ (donarse) a las asociaciones que **b** ____________ (dedicarse) a distribuir alimentos entre las personas sin recursos y los comedores sociales, según una estimación realizada por el Ministerio de Agricultura y la Federación Española de Bancos de Alimentos (Fesbal).

La ley no lo permite porque estas entidades no **c** ____________ (contar) con la infraestructura necesaria para su mantenimiento y distribución: furgonetas con equipo de frío y cámaras de almacenamiento, entre otros requisitos.

Sólo con los productos frescos de los supermercados que son desechados anualmente se **d** ____________ (poder) alimentar a unas 43.000 familias de cuatro miembros durante todo un año, calcula Fesbal.

La cifra de familias sin recursos **e** ____________ (atender) podría ser mucho mayor si **f** ____________ (sumar, nosotros) las toneladas de alimentos que sí pueden ser donados: legumbres, latas, aceite ..., pero que los comercios no ponen a disposición de las asociaciones por varios motivos: evitar que se **g** ____________ (aprovecharse) personas que no las necesitan y la molestia de tener que **h** ____________ (almacenar)las. Se calcula que por esta vía se despilfarran otras 357.000 toneladas al año.

Aunque está prohibido, varias asociaciones de barrios de Madrid, Barcelona y Bilbao **i** ____________ (recoger) desde hace tiempo los alimentos frescos de los supermercados y los **j** ____________ (distribuir) entre las familias que los necesitan.

Regular *-ar* verbs

infinitive	present	preterite	imperfect	future
hablar to speak	*hablo* *hablas* *habla* *hablamos* *habláis* *hablan*	*hablé* *hablaste* *habló* *hablamos* *hablasteis* *hablaron*	*hablaba* *hablabas* *hablaba* *hablábamos* *hablabais* *hablaban*	*hablaré* *hablarás* *hablará* *hablaremos* *hablaréis* *hablarán*

Regular *-er* verbs

infinitive	present	preterite	imperfect	future
comer to eat	*como* *comes* *come* *comemos* *coméis* *comen*	*comí* *comiste* *comió* *comimos* *comisteis* *comieron*	*comía* *comías* *comía* *comíamos* *comíais* *comían*	*comeré* *comerás* *comerá* *comeremos* *comeréis* *comerán*

Regular *-ir* verbs

infinitive	present	preterite	imperfect	future
vivir to live	*vivo* *vives* *vive* *vivimos* *vivís* *viven*	*viví* *viviste* *vivió* *vivimos* *vivisteis* *vivieron*	*vivía* *vivías* *vivía* *vivíamos* *vivíais* *vivían*	*viviré* *vivirás* *vivirá* *viviremos* *viviréis* *vivirán*

Irregular verbs

infinitive	present	preterite	imperfect	future
andar to walk	*ando* *andas* *anda* *andamos* *andáis* *andan*	*anduve* *anduviste* *anduvo* *anduvimos* *anduvisteis* *anduvieron*	*andaba* *andabas* *andaba* *andábamos* *andabais* *andaban*	*andaré* *andarás* *andará* *andaremos* *andaréis* *andarán*
caber to fit	*quepo* *cabes* *cabe* *cabemos* *cabéis* *caben*	*cupe* *cupiste* *cupo* *cupimos* *cupisteis* *cupieron*	*cabía* *cabías* *cabía* *cabíamos* *cabíais* *cabían*	*cabré* *cabrás* *cabrá* *cabremos* *cabréis* *cabrán*
caer to fall	*caigo* *caes* *cae* *caemos* *caéis* *caen*	*caí* *caíste* *cayó* *caímos* *caísteis* *cayeron*	*caía* *caías* *caía* *caíamos* *caíais* *caían*	*caeré* *caerás* *caerá* *caeremos* *caeréis* *caerán*
dar to give	*doy* *das* *da* *damos* *dais* *dan*	*di* *diste* *dio* *dimos* *disteis* *dieron*	*daba* *dabas* *daba* *dábamos* *dabais* *daban*	*daré* *darás* *dará* *daremos* *daréis* *darán*
decir to say	*digo* *dices* *dice* *decimos* *decís* *dicen*	*dije* *dijiste* *dijo* *dijimos* *dijisteis* *dijeron*	*decía* *decías* *decía* *decíamos* *decíais* *decían*	*diré* *dirás* *dirá* *diremos* *diréis* *dirán*
escribir to write	*escribo* *escribes* *escribe* *escribimos* *escribís* *escriben*	*escribí* *escribiste* *escribió* *escribimos* *escribisteis* *escribieron*	*escribía* *escribías* *escribía* *escribíamos* *escribíais* *escribían*	*escribiré* *escribirás* *escribirá* *escribiremos* *escribiréis* *escribirán*
estar to be	*estoy* *estás* *está* *estamos* *estáis* *están*	*estuve* *estuviste* *estuvo* *estuvimos* *estuvisteis* *estuvieron*	*estaba* *estabas* *estaba* *estábamos* *estabais* *estaban*	*estaré* *estarás* *estará* *estaremos* *estaréis* *estarán*

Irregular verbs (continued)

infinitive	present	preterite	imperfect	future
haber to have	*he* *has* *ha* *hemos* *habéis* *han*	*hube* *hubiste* *hubo* *hubimos* *hubisteis* *hubieron*	*había* *habías* *había* *habíamos* *habíais* *habían*	*habré* *habrás* *habrá* *habremos* *habréis* *habrá*
hacer to make	*hago* *haces* *hace* *hacemos* *hacéis* *hacen*	*hice* *hiciste* *hizo* *hicimos* *hicisteis* *hicieron*	*hacía* *hacías* *hacía* *hacíamos* *hacíais* *hacían*	*haré* *harás* *hará* *haremos* *haréis* *harán*
ir to go	*voy* *vas* *va* *vamos* *vais* *van*	*fui* *fuiste* *fue* *fuimos* *fuisteis* *fueron*	*iba* *ibas* *iba* *íbamos* *ibais* *iban*	*iré* *irás* *irá* *iremos* *iréis* *irán*
jugar to play	*juego* *juegas* *juega* *jugamos* *jugáis* *juegan*	*jugué* *jugaste* *jugó* *jugamos* *jugasteis* *jugaron*	*jugaba* *jugabas* *jugaba* *jugábamos* *jugabais* *jugaban*	*jugaré* *jugarás* *jugará* *jugaremos* *jugaréis* *jugarán*
leer to read	*leo* *lees* *lee* *leemos* *leéis* *leen*	*leí* *leíste* *leyó* *leímos* *leísteis* *leyeron*	*leía* *leías* *leía* *leíamos* *leíais* *leían*	*leeré* *leerás* *leerá* *leeremos* *leeréis* *leerán*
morir to die	*muero* *mueres* *muere* *morimos* *morís* *mueren*	*morí* *moriste* *murió* *morimos* *moristeis* *murieron*	*moría* *morías* *moría* *moríamos* *moríais* *morían*	*moriré* *morirás* *morirá* *moriremos* *moriréis* *morirán*
nacer to be born	*nazco* *naces* *nace* *nacemos* *nacéis* *nacen*	*nací* *naciste* *nació* *nacimos* *nacisteis* *nacieron*	*nacía* *nacías* *nacía* *nacíamos* *nacíais* *nacían*	*naceré* *nacerás* *nacerá* *naceremos* *naceréis* *nacerán*

Irregular verbs (continued)

infinitive	present	preterite	imperfect	future
poder to be able to	*puedo* *puedes* *puede* *podemos* *podéis* *pueden*	*pude* *pudiste* *pudo* *pudimos* *pudisteis* *pudieron*	*podía* *podías* *podía* *podíamos* *podíais* *podían*	*podré* *podrás* *podrá* *podremos* *podréis* *podrán*
poner to put	*pongo* *pones* *pone* *ponemos* *ponéis* *ponen*	*puse* *pusiste* *puso* *pusimos* *pusisteis* *pusieron*	*ponía* *ponías* *ponía* *poníamos* *poníais* *ponían*	*pondré* *pondrás* *pondrá* *pondremos* *pondréis* *pondrán*
querer to want	*quiero* *quieres* *quiere* *queremos* *queréis* *quieren*	*quise* *quisiste* *quiso* *quisimos* *quisisteis* *quisieron*	*quería* *querías* *quería* *queríamos* *queríais* *querían*	*querré* *querrás* *querrá* *querremos* *querréis* *querrán*
reír to laugh	*río* *ríes* *ríe* *reímos* *reís* *ríen*	*reí* *reíste* *rió* *reímos* *reísteis* *rieron*	*reía* *reías* *reía* *reíamos* *reíais* *reían*	*reiré* *reirás* *reirá* *reiremos* *reiréis* *reirán*
saber to know	*sé* *sabes* *sabe* *sabemos* *sabéis* *saben*	*supe* *supiste* *supo* *supimos* *supisteis* *supieron*	*sabía* *sabías* *sabía* *sabíamos* *sabíais* *sabían*	*sabré* *sabrás* *sabrá* *sabremos* *sabréis* *sabrán*
salir to leave	*salgo* *sales* *sale* *salimos* *salís* *salen*	*salí* *saliste* *salió* *salimos* *salisteis* *salieron*	*salía* *salías* *salía* *salíamos* *salíais* *salían*	*saldré* *saldrás* *saldrá* *saldremos* *saldréis* *saldrán*
ser to be	*soy* *eres* *es* *somos* *sois* *son*	*fui* *fuiste* *fue* *fuimos* *fuisteis* *fueron*	*era* *eras* *era* *éramos* *erais* *eran*	*seré* *serás* *será* *seremos* *seréis* *serán*

Irregular verbs (continued)

infinitive	present	preterite	imperfect	future
tener to have	*tengo* *tienes* *tiene* *tenemos* *tenéis* *tienen*	*tuve* *tuviste* *tuvo* *tuvimos* *tuvisteis* *tuvieron*	*tenía* *tenías* *tenía* *teníamos* *teníais* *tenían*	*tendré* *tendrás* *tendrá* *tendremos* *tendréis* *tendrán*
traer to bring	*traigo* *traes* *trae* *traemos* *traéis* *traen*	*traje* *trajiste* *trajo* *trajimos* *trajisteis* *trajeron*	*traía* *traías* *traía* *traíamos* *traíais* *traían*	*traeré* *traerás* *traerá* *traeremos* *traeréis* *traerán*
valer to be worth	*valgo* *vales* *vale* *valemos* *valéis* *valen*	*valí* *valiste* *valió* *valimos* *valisteis* *valieron*	*valía* *valías* *valía* *valíamos* *valíais* *valían*	*valdré* *valdrás* *valdrá* *valdremos* *valdréis* *valdrán*
venir to come	*vengo* *vienes* *viene* *venimos* *venís* *vienen*	*vine* *viniste* *vino* *vinimos* *vinisteis* *vinieron*	*venía* *venías* *venía* *veníamos* *veníais* *venían*	*vendré* *vendrás* *vendrá* *vendremos* *vendréis* *vendrán*
ver to see	*veo* *ves* *ve* *vemos* *veis* *ven*	*vi* *viste* *vio* *vimos* *visteis* *vieron*	*veía* *veías* *veía* *veíamos* *veíais* *veían*	*veré* *verás* *verá* *veremos* *veréis* *verá*

Transition

Nouns (page 5)

1

Masculine	Feminine
el sistema el problema el chico el traje el móvil el argumento el motor el ordenador	la calle la ciudad la cuestión la música la publicidad la ausencia la televisión

2
1 el, **2** la, **3** la, **4** la, **5** el, **6** el, **7** la, **8** el, **9** el, **10** el, **11** la, **12** la

Adjectives (page 6)

1
1 la televisión rota, **2** la emisión fascinante, **3** los peores resultados
4 las películas inolvidables, **5** los gatitos juguetones

2
1 los leones feroces, **2** los lugares preciosos, **3** las palabras incomprensibles, **4** las estudiantes trabajadoras, **5** los jugadores actuales

Definite and indefinite articles (page 7)

1
1**b**, 2**a**, 3**c**, 4**a**, 5**c**, 6**b**

2
1 los, **2** (no article before a profession), **3** los, **4** la, **5** unos
6 (no article before nationality), **7** una, **8** la

Word order (page 8)

1
1 Quiero comprar una televisión grande pronto.
2 Necesito ver la primera carrera esta tarde.
3 Es una película muy oscura con mucha violencia extrema.
4 En el futuro me gustaría ser un gran deportista.
5 Hay algunos chicos horribles en mi clase.
6 El antiguo jefe de la compañía lo anunció ayer.
7 Es de una familia bastante pobre.
8 Nadie ha considerado a los fabricantes mismos.
9 La primera vez vi algo increíble.
10 Quiero comprar esta silla antigua.
11 Hay algunos ejemplos evidentes.
12 Tiene los mismos problemas que nosotros.

The preterite tense (page 9)

1
1**b**, 2**c**, 3**b**, 4**c**, 5**c**

2

Across
2. contestó
5. dijo
8. aprendió
11. asumí
13. interrumpió
14. tuvo
15. celebró
17. vi
18. fui

Down
1. dependió
3. confirmé
4. rompí
6. permitió
7. escribí
9. quiso
10. hizo
12. sorprendió
13. ignoró
16. bailé
18. fue

The imperfect tense (page 10)

1a and **b**

Number	T / F	Correction?
1	F	It refers to the past.
2	F	The first step is to remove the infinitive ending (*-ar*, *-er* or *-ir*).
3	T	
4	F	*-ía* is the ending for *-er* or *-ir* verbs. *-aba* is the 'I' form ending for *-ar* verbs.
5	T	
6	F	There are only three irregulars, but they are *ir*, *ser* and ***ver***.

The conditional tense (page 11)

1a
Me gustaría, Sería, Se debería, Visitaría, Volvería

1b
tenía, comí, hago

1c
1 gustar, **2** ser, **3** tener, **4** comer, **5** deber, **6** visitar, **7** hacer, **8** volver

1d
1 tendría, **2** comería, **3** haría

The immediate future tense (page 12)

1
1 f, **2** g, **3** b, **4** e, **5** a, **6** h, **7** c, **8** d

2

1 voy a leer		**a** *I am going to read*
2 vamos a ver		**b** *we are going to see*
3 van a decir		**c** *they are going to say*
4 vais a jugar		**d** *you (pl.) are going to play*
5 vas a bailar		**e** *you are going to dance*
6 va a ser		**f** *it is going to be*
7 voy a ayudar		**g** *I am going to help*
8 vamos a ir		**h** *we are going to go*

Negatives and infinitive constructions (page 13)

1
1 Nadie, **2** nada, **3** ni ... ni, **4** Tampoco

2
1 No hay nadie mejor – *There is no-one better.*
2 Nunca voy a la piscina pequeña – *I never go to the small pool.*
3 No quiero nada más tampoco – *I don't want anything else either.*
4 No fui al centro con mis amigos – *I didn't go to the centre with my friends.*
5 No tengo ningún disco nuevo – *I have no new disks.*

3
1 Va a ser importante estudiar más.
2 Para mejorar las notas tengo que prestar atención.
3 Acabo de leer un libro en español, ¡y he mejorado mi vocabulario!
4 Al empezar el curso decidí estudiar bien la gramática.

Topic 1

Gustar (page 14)

1
1 nos, **2** les, **3** le, **4** os, **5** me, **6** te, **7** le, **8** les

2
1**c**, 2**a**, 3**e**, 4**b**, 5**d**

3
1 I've got ten left over.
2 It interested you a lot.

3 They would be interested in knowing a bit more.
4 Me gustan.
5 Nos sobran algunas galletas.
6 Le encantaba.
7 Me duelen.
8 Me gustó.

Por or *para*? (page 15)

1

1 *para* = for (somebody) (7)
2 *para* = in order to (intention) (8)
3 *por* = due to (1)
4 *por* = through (movement) (3)
5 *por* = due to (1)
6 *por* = through (movement) (3), *para* = in order to (intention) (8)
7 *para* = for (somebody) (7), *para* = in order to (intention) (8)
8 *para* = purpose (7)

2

1 por, 2 por, para, 3 para, para, 4 por, para, 5 por, 6 para

Standard Spanish endings (page 16)

1

1 la imaginación (Note the definite article.)
2 necesario (Remember, 'ss' does not happen in Spanish!)
3 una situación
4 una comunidad (Remember, 'mm' does not happen in Spanish!)
5 un fanático
6 eléctrico
7 un cliente
8 sarcástico
9 generalmente
10 una diferencia (Remember, 'ff' does not happen in Spanish!)
11 un constante
12 la tolerancia (Note the definite article.)
13 la importancia
14 relevante
15 ambicioso

Comparatives and superlatives (page 17)

1

1 mejor, **2** más, **3** como, **4** tanta, **5** que, **6** el, **7** de, **8** las, **9** menor, mejor, **10** tan

Ser and *estar* (page 18)

1

Estar		*Ser*				
Location	Temporary state	Identity	Possession	Time	Fact	With infinitive
4 8	1 3	9	10	12	2 5 6 7	11

2a and **b**

1 Son – *It's 3.30 in Spain.*
2 está, es – *Pepe is in a bad mood, he's / it's really annoying.*
3 Era, estaba, es – *I was an engineer but it was boring / I was bored – it's a difficult job.*
4 Estoy, es, es – *I am in Buenos Aires: it's the capital of Argentina and it's a lovely city.*
5 es, es – *Your answer is wrong – it's important to check what you have written.*
6 estar – *They should be studying and not playing football.*
7 es, es – *The table is made of wood and it's very cheap.*
8 Somos, es – *We are fans of heavy metal music, but according to my parents it's a phase.*

3

1 Soy, **2** Estaba, **3** Es, **4** eran, **5** Estoy, estaba, **6** Estaré

The present tense (page 19)

1

	aprovechar (to make the most of)	***temer*** (to fear)	***decidir*** (to decide)
I	aprovecho	temo	decido
you	aprovechas	temes	decides
he / she / it / you (formal)	aprovecha	teme	decide
we	aprovechamos	tememos	decidimos
you (plural)	aprovecháis	teméis	decidís
they / you (plural, formal)	aprovechan	temen	deciden

2a and **b**

	Conjugated verb	Infinitive
1	creo	creer
2	tiene	tener
3	se levantan	levantarse
4	ponen	poner
5	debemos	deber
6	es	ser
7	quieren	querer
8	ofrece	ofrecer
9	faltan	faltar
10	salen	salir

2c Students' own answers.

Irregular present tense verbs (page 20)

1

1 esperan, **2** veo, **3** tenemos, **4** haces, **5** envían, **6** sé, **7** decidimos, **8** lee, **9** compran, **10** sale

Impersonal *se* and passive (page 21)

1

1 Se opina (impersonal)
2 Se puede (impersonal)
3 Se debe (impersonal)
4 Se venden (passive)
5 Se vivía (impersonal)
6 Se hablan (passive)
7 se prohíbe (passive)
8 se escribe (impersonal)
9 se viajará (impersonal)
10 se sigue (impersonal)

2

1 ¿Cómo se dice 'terrified' en español?
2 Se pagan unas multas enormes cada año.
3 Se alquilan bicicletas en la tienda cerca del río.
4 Se puede visitar el museo y la catedral.
5 Cada tarde se va al café para hablar de la política.
6 En el instituto local se ofrecen muchos cursos interesantes para los mayores.
7 En el restaurante al lado de la estación se sirve una sopa de pescado deliciosa.
8 Lo siento, el pastel se terminó ayer.

Lo with an adjective or an adverb (page 22)

1

1 Entrenaba lo más duro **posible.**
2 Decidió que lo **peligroso** sería ignorarlo.
3 Lo **divertido** era el parque acuático.
4 Lo **interesante** es que nadie sabe la verdad.
5 Quiere mejorar lo más **rápidamente posible**.

6 Lo **importante** del problema es que afecta a mucha gente.
7 Se debería cambiar **lo más pronto posible**.
8 Todos los concursantes quieren hacer lo **mejor posible**.

2
1 The dangerous thing about this situation is also its most attractive feature.
2 The worrying thing is that nobody called me.
3 You should buy something as fast / as soon as possible.
4 The advisable thing would be to finish the work immediately.
5 The good thing is that it didn't cause much damage.
6 He / She always drives as efficiently as possible.
7 It's the ugliest that I've seen in my life.
8 The fundamental thing is to prepare yourself thoroughly / rigorously.

Disjunctive pronouns (page 23)

1
1c, 2d, 3a, 4b, 5f, 6h, 7e, 8g

2
1 para ti, 2 para ella, 3 con ellos, 4 al lado de usted, 5 con él, 6 para nosotros, 7 para ustedes, 8 para ello

Mixed practice (page 24)

1 Students' own answers.

2
1 Lo más, más
2 bueno, se, más
3 está, malo, por
4 Queremos, para, por
5 Te sobran, Quiero

3
1 Seguimos el mejor consejo de los expertos.
2 Lo peor cuando salgo con mis amigos es cuánto gastamos.
3 ¿Os gusta lo que veis?
4 Vamos a una playa aislada – para mi es la más bonita.
5 No se debe comprar ni los productos más populares ni los más caros.
6 Es una emisión clásica pero no nos gusta para nada.
7 Están en Barcelona en uno de los hoteles más baratos.
8 Nos quedan dos días antes de la noche más divertida de nuestras vidas.

Test yourself (page 25)

1
J está, B habla, L más, E que, D por, H para, A ser

2a and **b**
1 Lamentablemente yo no **puedo** ir contigo – **hago** mucho deporte cada fin de semana.
Unfortunately I can't go with you – I do lots of sport every weekend.
2 Mi padre **utiliza** una tableta pero yo **sigo** utilizando este ordenador viejo.
My father uses a modern tablet but I'm still using this old computer.
3 Normalmente yo **compro** productos reciclados pero no se **venden** muchos en mi pueblo.
Normally I buy recycled products but they don't sell many in my town.
4 En mi opinión **vemos** demasiada telebasura pero nos **encanta**.
In my opinion we watch too much rubbish on TV but we love it.
5 Mi hermano **está** en Madrid por trabajo durante casi un mes, pero nuestros primos **viven** allí también.
My brother is in Madrid for work for almost a month, but our cousins live there too.

Topic 2
Demonstrative adjectives and pronouns (page 26)

1
1 Ese, esta, 2 Estos, 3 esos, estos, 4 Esta, 5 Esas

2
Éste es un problema que no se debe ignorar. **Estas** noticias recientes sobre el cambio climático son muy graves, y no se puede decir que son "**aquellos**" científicos o políticos los que tienen la responsabilidad de solucionar **esta** situación. **Ese** argumento no sirve para nada. **Éste** es nuestro planeta, ¿pero dónde está nuestro plan?

More on the preterite tense (page 27)

1

apoyar	*to support*	prometer	*to promise*	decidir	*to decide*
apoyé	*I supported*	prometí	*I promised*	decidí	*I decided*
apoyaste	*you supported*	prometiste	*you promised*	decidiste	*you decided*
apoyó	*he / she / you (formal) supported*	prometió	*he / she / you (formal) promised*	decidió	*he / she / you (formal) decided*
apoyamos	*we supported*	prometimos	*we promised*	decidimos	*we decided*
apoyasteis	*you (pl.) supported*	prometisteis	*you (pl.) promised*	decidisteis	*you (pl.) decided*
apoyaron	*they / you (pl. formal) supported*	prometieron	*they / you (pl. formal) promised*	decidieron	*they / you (pl. formal) decided*

2
1 hablaron – they / you (pl. formal) spoke
2 volví – I returned
3 descansamos – we relaxed
4 temió – he / she / it / you (formal) feared
5 permitisteis – you (pl.) allowed
6 fui – I went
7 definiste – you defined
8 dependió – he / she / it / you (formal) depended
9 lucharon – they / you (pl. formal) fought
10 cambié – I changed

3 Students' own answers.

More on the imperfect tense (page 28)

1a and **b**
1 existir, we were existing / used to exist
2 averiguar, I / he / she / you (formal) was / were finding out
3 suceder, it was happening
4 correr, you were running / used to run
5 añadir, they / you (pl formal) were adding / used to add
6 aprovechar, I / he / she / you (formal) used to make the most of
7 ocurrir, it was occurring / used to occur
8 sorprender, you were surprising / used to surprise
9 jurar, we were swearing / used to swear
10 emitir, they were emitting / used to emit / were broadcasting / used to broadcast

2 Students' own answers.

The perfect tense (page 29)

1
1 hecho (irregular), 2 cumplido, 3 admitido, 4 cubierto (similar to descubrir), 5 luchado, 6 vuelto (irregular), 7 combatido, 8 disuadido, 9 permitido

2
1 he salido, 2 hemos luchado, 3 has prometido, 4 ¿habéis recibido?, 5 han abierto, 6 ha adoptado, 7 ha muerto, 8 he dicho

3 Students' own answers.

The present continuous (page 30)

1
1 fingiendo, 2 viendo, 3 decidiendo, 4 explicando, 5 protegiendo, 6 investigando, 7 haciendo, 8 intentando, 9 siguiendo

2

1 Estoy intentando explicar los problemas principales.
2 Están tomando un café en el centro.
3 Nos gusta ir a ver partidos a menudo.
4 Sigue interrumpiéndome.
5 ¿Estás practicando lo suficiente?
6 Está mejorando pero debe seguir estudiando.

Direct and indirect object pronouns (page 31)

1

1d Porque no **os** vimos – no hay otra razón, **os lo** prometo.
2b Claro, **se lo** di ayer.
3f **Me** encantan, pero creo que tiene una imaginación rarísima.
4a Sí – todavía no **la** he llamado pero quiero ver**la** pronto.
5e Mi vecino **me lo** enseñó – es argentino.
6c Lamentablemente no **nos** invitaron, pero **les** voy a enviar algo.

Personal 'a' (page 32)

1

1a, 2a, 3a, 4b, 5a

2

1 No conozco **a** nadie que sepa tocar la guitarra.
2 Voy al parque con mis amigos.
3 Sí, Juanma pegó **a** Pepe fuera de la discoteca.
4 Necesito un fontanero que trabaje los fines de semana.
5 ¿Recuerdas la película de que me hablaste? La vi y no la recomendaría **a** nadie.

3

1 Busco a alguien para compartir piso.
2 Tenemos ocho gatos y tres perros.
3 No vi a nadie ayer, tuve que trabajar.
4 Este verano quiero ir de vacaciones con mi familia.
5 Necesito algo un poco más complicado.
6 Anoche conocí a la chica de mis sueños.

The subjunctive (page 33)

1

1 cambie, **2** tengas, **3** admitamos, **4** pueda, **5** duerma

When to use the subjunctive (page 34)

1a and **b**

1	quiera	SUBJ
2	seáis	SUBJ
3	hayan	SUBJ
4	espero poder ir	NO SUBJ – no change of subject
5	compres	SUBJ
6	olvides	SUBJ
7	escondan	SUBJ
8	practicar	NO SUBJ – *es importante* + infinitive
9	tengas	SUBJ
10	es	NO SUBJ – *no creo que* would need subjunctive, but *creo que* is stating what you think to be fact.

More on *ser* and *estar* (page 35)

1

ser	estar
estudiante alto francés	en Egipto enferma viviendo

2

El chico estaba listo. También era un joven bueno y considerado, pero estaba aburrido de su vida cotidiana y quería ver el mundo.

Mixed practice (page 36)

1

infinitive	I	you	he / she / it / you (formal)	we	you (pl.)	they / you (pl. formal)
1 temer	tema	temas	tema	temamos	temáis	teman
2 permitir	permita	permitas	permita	permitamos	permitáis	permitan
3 querer	quiera	quieras	quiera	queramos	queráis	quieran
4 mostrar	muestre	muestres	muestre	mostremos	mostréis	muestren
5 empezar	empiece	empieces	empiece	empecemos	empecéis	empiecen
6 ver	vea	veas	vea	veamos	veáis	vean
7 saber	sepa	sepas	sepa	sepamos	sepáis	sepan

2a

1 me gusta (present), voy (present), es (present)
2 Creo (present), continuarán (future)
3 iba (imperfect)
4 era (imperfect), me gustaba (imperfect)
5 tengo (present), me apetece (present), soy (present)
6 se murió (preterite), tenía (imperfect)

2b

4, 6, 3, 1, 2, 5

2c

When I was young I used to like going to the cinema with my father to watch cartoons. But he died when I was twelve years old. Until that moment I always went with him. But now I love going with my girlfriend and at times I go alone, it's very relaxing. I believe that my tastes, with regards to films, will continue changing in the next few years. I also really want to take my son to the cinema – but I don't fancy being a Dad in the near future, I'm still too young.

Test yourself (page 37)

1

1 Te recomendamos que **compres** un traje nuevo; **ése** no te queda muy bien.
2 **Queríamos** ir al cine ayer pero Juan **tuvo** que ir al médico.
3 **Estamos** cansados y **sería** casi imposible terminar el trabajo hoy.
4 ¿En serio? No **estoy** de acuerdo. **Era** mejor cuando teníamos veinte años.
5 Estaba **explicándoselo** a Laly cuando el teléfono **sonó**.
6 ¿**Habéis terminado** todos? **Seguís** hablando pero no me gusta para nada.

2

D utilizando, **K** ha sido, **E** registró, **F** estas, **C** este, **H** acompañada, **A** indicativos

Topic 3

The conditional tense (page 38)

1

1 gustaría, **2** cambiaríamos, **3** Habría, **4** diría, **5** podría

2 Students' own answers.

Radical-changing present tense verbs (page 39)

1

dormir (*to sleep*) jugar (*to play*) recomendar (*to recommend*)

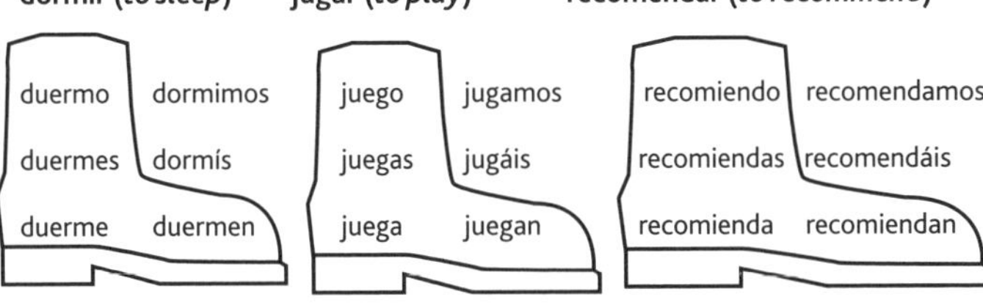

2a and **b**	**infinitive**	**meaning**
1 vierten	vertir	to pour out
2 recuerdo	recordar	to remember
3 confiesa	confesar	to confess
4 consienten	consentir	to consent
5 miento	mentir	to lie

3

1 El chico niega las acusaciones.
2 Suelo ir al cine cada semana.
3 Empieza a las ocho y las puertas se cierran a las ocho y diez.
4 Recomendamos escucharlo, es fenomenal.
5 Enciendo la luz porque quiero ver más.

The pluperfect tense (page 40)

1

English	Spanish	English	Spanish
I had bought	había comprado	*we had bought*	habíamos comprado
you had bought	habías comprado	*you (pl.) had bought*	habíais comprado
he / she / you (formal) had bought	había comprado	*they / you (pl. formal) had bought*	habían comprado

2

English	Spanish	English	Spanish
I had pretended	había fingido	*we had pretended*	habíamos fingido
you had pretended	habías fingido	*you (pl.) had pretended*	habíais fingido
he / she / you (formal) had pretended	había fingido	*they / you (pl. formal) had pretended*	habían fingido

3a

1 dicho, **2** bebido, **3** completado, **4** abolido, **5** vuelto, **6** visto

3b Students' own answers.

4 Students' own answers.

Hace ... que and *desde hace* (page 41)

1a and **b**

1 **Hace** tres años fui a España por primera vez.
Three years ago I went to Spain for the first time.
2 **Hace** dos meses **que** no veo a Juan.
It's two months since I've seen Juan.
3 Estudié francés **durante** casi cinco años, pero no me gustó mucho.
I studied French for almost five years, but I didn't like it much.
4 Ahorro **desde hace** muchos años para ir de vacaciones.
I've been saving for many years to go on holiday.
5 Quería visitar Ecuador **desde** la infancia.
I had wanted to visit Ecuador since childhood.
6 Buscaba trabajo **desde** que había terminado los estudios.
I had been looking for a job since finishing my studies.
7 Los terminé **hace** tres meses.
I finished them three months ago.
8 **Hace** mucho tiempo que no salgo con mis amigos porque me preparo para la carrera de este viernes.
It's been a long time since I've been out with my friends because I'm preparing myself for the race on Friday.

Reflexive verbs (page 42)

1

meterse – *to get involved in* PRETERITE			
Singular	Meaning	Plural	Meaning
me **metí**	***I got involved in***	**nos metimos**	***we got involved in***
te metiste	*you got involved in*	os **metisteis**	***you (pl.) got involved in***
se metió	***he / she / you (formal) got involved in***	**se metieron**	*they / you (pl. formal) got involved in*

2a and **b**

1 present. (Note: Students may suggest the preterite here as the form *levantamos* is the same as the present. However, the word *normalmente* makes it clear the reference is to a habitual action, so if talking about the past the imperfect *levantábamos* would be used.)
Normalmente me levanto bastante tarde.
2 preterite
No nos dimos cuenta de la situación hasta ayer.
3 imperfect
¿Te dormías durante la película?
4 immediate future
¿Vais a poneros un abrigo? Está lloviendo.
5 conditional
Me sentiría mejor después de una siesta, seguro.

Imperatives (page 43)

1a

	hablarle – *to talk to her*			
	tú	vosotros	usted	ustedes
positive	háblale	habladle	háblele	háblenle
negative	no le hables	no le habléis	no le hable	no le hablen

1b

	decírmelo – *to say it to me*			
	tú	vosotros	usted	ustedes
positive	dímelo	decídmelo	dígamelo	díganmelo
negative	no me lo digas	no me lo digáis	no me lo diga	no me lo digan

	cerrarlo – *to close it*			
	tú	vosotros	usted	ustedes
positive	ciérralo	cerradlo	ciérrelo	ciérrenlo
negative	no lo cierres	no lo cerréis	no lo cierre	no lo cierren

Irregular preterites (pages 44–45)

1

1 estuve, **2** advertí, **3** empecé, **4** tuve, **5** di, **6** busqué, **7** adiviné **8** sugerí, **9** dije, **10** volví

2a

Regular	Irregular	Spelling change in 1st person preterite	Radical-changing 3rd person preterite
terminar	ir	jugar	elegir
aprovechar	ser	pagar	consentir
abrir	hacer	tocar	conseguir

2b Students' own answers.

3 Students' own answers.

4 Students' own answers.

The future tense (pages 46–47)

1a–d

	Future tense	Meaning	Infinitive
1	comerás	*you will eat*	comer
2	dirán	*they / you (pl. formal) will say*	decir
3	viviré	*I will live*	vivir
4	querremos	*we will want*	querer
5	alquilaré	*I will hire / rent*	alquilar
6	dependerá	*he / she / it / you (formal) will depend*	depender
7	sorprenderéis	*you (pl.) will surprise*	sorprender
8	aclararé	*I will clarify / explain*	aclarar
9	habrá	*there will be*	haber
10	recibiremos	*we will receive*	recibir

2

1 En junio todos **tendréis** que hacer el examen – **será** importante sacar buenas notas.
2 Te **veré** mañana e **iremos** a la biblioteca – necesito tu ayuda.
3 ¿Cuándo **llegarán**? Les **llamaremos** a las cinco para saber los detalles. (Note: the *les* informs you that the 'you' who is arriving is plural and in the *ustedes* form.)
4 En el futuro **lograrás** mucho pero antes **hará** falta esforzarte un poco más.
5 **Podremos** utilizar fuentes de energía menos nocivas, algo que **protegerá** el futuro del planeta para nuestros hijos.

3 Students' own answers.

Mixed practice (pages 48–49)

1a–d

Pluperfect x 2	Imperfect x 3	Preterite x 5	Present x 5	Future x 2	Conditional x 3
verb: había visto ***inf:*** ver ***trans:*** I / he / she / you (formal) had seen ***verb:*** habíais ido ***inf:*** ir ***trans:*** you had gone	***verb:*** comían ***inf:*** comer ***trans:*** they / you (pl. formal) were eating ***verb:*** adivinaba inf: adivinar ***trans:*** I / he / she / you (formal) were guessing ***verb:*** querías inf: querer ***trans:*** you wanted / used to want	***verb:*** fuiste ***inf:*** ir / ser ***trans:*** you went / were ***verb:*** vio ***inf:*** ver trans: he / she / you (formal) saw ***verb:*** cubrió ***inf:*** cubrir ***trans:*** he / she / it / you (formal) covered ***verb:*** escribí ***inf:*** escribir ***trans:*** I wrote ***verb:*** subieron ***inf:*** subir ***trans:*** they went up	***verb:*** juego ***inf:*** jugar ***trans:*** I play ***verb:*** merezco ***inf:*** merecer ***trans:*** I deserve verb: huele ***inf:*** oler ***trans:*** he / she / it / you (formal) smell(s) ***verb:*** prefiere ***inf:*** preferir ***trans:*** he / she / it / you (formal) prefer(s) ***verb:*** piensan ***inf:*** pensar ***trans:*** they think	***verb:*** diremos ***inf:*** decir ***trans:*** we will say ***verb:*** valdrá ***inf:*** valer ***trans:*** it will be worth	***verb:*** querrías ***inf:*** querer ***trans:*** you would want ***verb:*** tendrían ***inf:*** tener ***trans:*** they / you (pl. formal) would want ***verb:*** prepararía ***inf:*** preparar ***trans:*** I / he / she / you (formal) would prepare

1e Students' own answers.

2a–2c Students' own answers.

Test yourself (pages 50–51)

1

G estas, **J** obtendrán, **E** la, **B** Hace, **F** estableció, **H** por, **D** proviene, **A** relacionadas

2

I que, **E** pidieron, **J** acabe, **H** sucedió, **L** quien, **C** dijo, **B** cerraran

Topic 4

Possessive adjectives and pronouns (page 52)

1a and **b**

1	vuestra mentalidad	your mentality
2	mis problemas	my problems
3	tu perfil	your profile
4	nuestras opiniones	our opinions
5	vuestra crisis	your crisis

2a and **b**

1 Mi familia vivía al lado de la suya en Madrid.
My family used to live next to his in Madrid.
2 Había dejado mi coche cerca del tuyo.
I had left my car next to yours.
3 Su equipo juega en la misma liga que la nuestra.
His team plays in the same league as ours.
4 Nadie niega que son suyas.
Nobody denies that they are his / hers / yours / theirs.
5 El problema es que he perdido los míos.
The problem is that I've lost mine.

6 Deberíais daros cuenta de la diferencia entre los tuyos y los suyos.
You should realise / understand the difference between yours and his / hers / theirs.
7 No creo que mis opiniones sean tan firmes como las tuyas.
I don't think my opinions are as strong as yours.
8 Ha utilizado la mía desde que empezó en junio.
He has been using mine since he began in June.

Relative pronouns and adjectives (pages 53–54)

1

Relative pronoun or adjective	Usage
que	Refers to people or things Can be used either as a subject or object pronoun
quien	Only refers to people Used after prepositions *a*, *de*, *en* and *con*
el que etc.	Used when *que* might be ambiguous
el cual etc.	Used after all prepositions except *a*, *de*, *en* and *con*
lo que	Used to describe an abstract, general concept
cuyo etc.	'Whose' Sentence contains an owner and something owned Agrees with the owned noun

2
1e, **2**b, **3**d, **4**f, **5**a, **6**c

3
1 Es la casa en la cual nadie ha entrado desde 1978.
2 ¡Mira quién llega!
3 Hay muchas cosas que puedes hacer.
4 Por desgracia lo que quiero hacer es imposible.
5 Mi amigo, que vivía en la casa al lado de la tuya, ahora vive en España.
6 Mis dos amigos, los que acaban de casarse, han decidido visitar a mi tío, cuya casa es enorme.

When to use subjunctives (page 55)

1a and **b**
1 envíen: wish + change of subject
2 vayamos: expression of purpose
3 llegues, veas: *cuando* + reference to future event, recommendation
4 compre, depende (**not subjunctive**), debemos (**not subjunctive**): doubt (*tal vez*), no subject introducer / change of subject, no subject introducer / change of subject
5 digan, digan, tengo: set phrase, set phrase, positive use of *creo que* (not used in a questioning sense: *no creo que* would have required a subjunctive)

2a
1 aconseje, **2** den, **3** empecemos, **4** prometas, **5** quiera, **6** vayáis, **7** fuerce, **8** ignores

2b Students' own answers.

Avoiding the passive (page 56)

1
1 Unos expertos han organizado la conferencia.
2 Los romanos destruyeron la ciudad hace casi dos mil años.
3 Se perdió como resultado de unos errores graves.
4 Uno de nuestros agentes locales lo entregará el lunes.
5 Le ha visitado tanta gente que ahora está demasiado cansado.
6 Se detuvo a alguien esta mañana, aunque la policía protege su identidad.
7 Una compañía local patrocina al equipo.
8 Los aduaneros nos pararon y examinaron nuestras maletas.

Past tenses – when do you use each one? (page 57)

1a and **b**

	Perfect	Imperfect	Preterite	Pluperfect
Verb	ha aprovechado	añadíamos	vivieron	habían asistido
Translation	*he / she / it / you (formal) has / have made the most of*	*we were adding / used to add*	*they / you (pl. formal) lived*	*they / you (pl. formal) had attended*
Verb	hemos persuadido	bailabas	destruyó	habías hecho
Translation	*we have persuaded*	*you used to dance / were dancing*	*he / she / it / you (formal) destroyed*	*you had done*
Verb		existía	supiste	
Translation		*I / he / she / it / you (formal) used to exist*	*you knew*	

2a–c
1 *fui* – preterite – completed action, not recent; *nos encontramos* – preterite – completed action, not recent; *habíamos visto* – pluperfect – step further back in time compared to the preterite events
2 *Me entrenaba* – imperfect – ongoing action; *me torcí* – preterite – completed action, interrupting the imperfect action; *tuve* – preterite – completed action, not recent
3 *he organizado* – perfect – completed, recent action (implies the organisation was going on until very recently); *llamé* – preterite – completed action, completed before the organising was finished; *ha dado* – perfect – completed, recent action
4 *han probado* – perfect – completed action, but no definite time given – ongoing until recently

The imperfect subjunctive (pages 58–59)

1

Infinitive	3rd person plural of preterite	Remove -ron	Form imperfect subjunctive requested
bailar	**bailaron**	**baila**	**(yo) bailara**
vivir	vivieron	vivie	(tú) vivieras
ganar	ganaron	gana	(vosotras) ganarais
poder	pudieron	pudie	(ellos) pudieran
querer	quisieron	quisie	(él) quisiera
ser	fueron	fue	(nosotros) fuéramos
tocar	tocaron	toca	(usted) tocara
dormir	durmieron	durmie	(ustedes) durmieran
seguir	siguieron	siguie	(ella) siguiera
comprender	comprendieron	comprendie	(yo) comprendiera
existir	existieron	existie	(él) existiera

2
1 Si **pudiera** elegir, **preferiría** ir al Caribe.
2 Creo que mi hermano **buscaría** otro trabajo si **tuviera** más confianza.
3 **Iría** de compras si **ganara** un poco más de dinero.
4 Si mis amigos **supieran** la verdad, **sería** un alivio enorme.
5 **Viviría** aquí con nosotros si **consiguiera** los papeles.
6 **Yo me casaría** con ella si **pudiera**.
7 Si **estudiaran** aun un poco más, me parece que sus notas **mejorarían** rápidamente.

8 Aunque me llevo bastante bien con mis padres, nos **llevaríamos** mejor si **hubiera** un poco más de espacio en casa.
9 **Se enfadaría** mucho si **perdiera** el móvil; siempre lo lleva consigo y lo usa casi sin parar.
10 Si **dejaras** de envenenarte con el tabaco **te sentirías** más sano y **tendrías** mucho más dinero porque no **gastarías** tanto cada semana en comprar cigarrillos.

Subjunctives in different tenses (page 60)

1

Across
1. hubiéramos comido
4. hubieras visto
6. juegue
7. dudo que
10. haya terminado
11. vuelva
12. no creo que
13. para que

Down
1. hayan hecho
2. comierais
3. hayas dicho
5. fuera
8. recomiendo que
9. vaya

2 Possible answers include:
1 hayas cambiado, **2** llamaras, **3** hubieran preparado, **4** vengan, hagas, hagas, **5** des, **6** hayan decidido, **7** dijeras, **8** estudiara

Indefinite adjectives and pronouns (page 61)

1
1c, 2d, 3a, 4e, 5b

2
1 alguien, **2** Algo, **3** Ningún, **4** tan, **5** algunos, **6** Mucha, **7** otro

Recognising the future perfect and conditional perfect tenses (page 62)

1a–c
1 habremos terminado, FP, We will have finished before 8, I swear to you.
2 habrían continuado, CP, They would have continued but the rain was too heavy.
3 habríamos ganado, CP, We would have won if the referee had understood the rules.
4 te habrían respetado, CP, They would have respected you more if you had not been so rude / badly behaved.
5 yo te habría dejado, CP, I would have left you years ago but you needed my help.
6 habréis conocido, FP, You will have got to know a lot of people on your travels.

2

Future	Conditional	Future perfect	Conditional perfect
vivirán tendrán	sería me gustaría pondríais	habrá llegado habré comido habremos visto	habríamos sido habría terminado

Mixed practice (page 63)

1
1 If my parents were to divorce I would have to decide who to live with.
2 We will go out when you've finished your homework.
3 The cyclist hadn't taken any illegal substances.
4 We haven't eaten in that restaurant for many months.
5 Not even in my dreams would I have imagined living in such a beautiful place.
6 I was going to school when I saw the accident. I heard some horrifying screams.
7 It's essential that you admit the truth so that we can change the policy.

2
1 Creo que el divorcio es demasiado fácil hoy en día.
2 Si alguien atacara a mi hermano querría venganza.
3 Aquélla es la chica cuyos hermanos están la cárcel.
4 Digan lo que digan, quiero que sigas tus deseos – esta vida es muy corta.
5 En el pasado nadie hablaba del turismo sostenible pero es esencial para la supervivencia de muchas partes del planeta.
6 Ojalá fuera posible en la vida real – desafortunadamente nadie me ha pedido la misma cosa.

3 Students' own answers.

Test yourself (page 64–65)

1
A está, **D** sufran, **H** admitiendo, **G** fueramos, **E** conseguiríamos, **C** duerman, **I** realicen

2
a se donen, **b** se dedican, **c** cuentan, **d** puede / podría, **e** atendidas, **f** sumáramos, **g** aprovechen, **h** almacenarlas, **i** recogen, **j** distribuyen

The author and the publisher would like to thank and acknowledge the following for the use of their material:

p37 Adapted from http://www.20minutos.com.mx/noticia/2104/0/artico/volumen/superficie/, accessed 20 February 2013.

p50 Adapted from http://www.20minutos.es/noticia/1585758/0/reducir-sal/beneficios/como-dejar-tabaco/, accessed 20 February 2013.

p51 Adapted from http://www.20minutos.com.mx/noticia/2123/0/minifalda/diputada/crystal-tovar/, accessed 20 February 2013.

p64 Adapted from http://www.20minutos.es/noticia/1481178/0/comer-en-familia/prevenir/trastornos-alimenticios/, accessed 20 February 2013.

p65 Adapted from http://www.20minutos.es/noticia/1596371/0/supermercados/comida/basura/, accessed 20 February 2013.

Every effort has been made to trace the copyright holders but if any have been inadvertently overlooked the publisher will be pleased to make the necessary amendments or arrangements at the first opportunity.